IN FREE FALL

IN FREE FALL
My Experiments with Living

MALLIKA SARABHAI

Illustrations by Priyankar Gupta

SPEAKING TIGER BOOKS LLP
125A, Ground Floor, Shahpur Jat, near Asiad Village,
New Delhi 110049

First published by Speaking Tiger Books 2022

Text copyright © Mallika Sarabhai 2022
Illustrations copyright © Priyankar Gupta 2022

ISBN: 978-93-5447-096-7
eISBN: 978-93-5447-104-9

10 9 8 7 6 5 4 3 2 1

Typeset in Adobe Garamond Pro by SŪRYA, New Delhi
Printed at ...

All rights reserved.
No part of this publication may be reproduced, transmitted, or stored in a retrieval system, in any form or by any means, electronic, mechanical, photocopying, recording or otherwise, without the prior permission of the publisher.

This book is sold subject to the condition that it shall not, by way of trade or otherwise, be lent, resold, hired out, or otherwise circulated, without the publisher's prior consent, in any form of binding or cover other than that in which it is published.

To

Freddie
Seetamma
Tipki
Sukhi
Bolki
Chupki
Maya
Anna
Kanha
Panchali
Uttara
Choros
Cleo
Socrates
Neera
Gutlus
Begum
Noor
and Golmol

My beloved four-legged friends who never stop wanting and loving me.

CONTENTS

Foreword by Dr Jamuna Pai   ix

Introduction: In Search of a Holistic Life   xi
by Dr Issac Mathai

1. How It All Began   1
2. Every Diet Is Worth a Try   8
3. Inside Outside   21
4. The Smoking Gun and Other Addictions   28
5. Finding Dance and Yoga   40
6. The Empty Sella   49
7. Dancing My Way Through Pregnancy   65
8. Training Tiny Muscles   76
9. A Coloured Life   85

10. Mudslinging	100
11. With a Little Help from My Friends	108
12. Healing Others	133
13. Unmessing My Head	145
14. Occupying My Body, Making It My Friend: The Last Twenty Years	155
Epilogue: The Comeuppance	160
Acknowledgements	166
Appendix: My Daily Yoga Asanas	167
Bibliography	191

Foreword

Over the three decades that I have known Mallika, initially as a client, and then as a friend whose friendship I value, I have always been struck by her zest for life, her clear thinking mind and her capacity to adapt herself to changing situations. Her ability to take charge of the various challenges life throws at her, and turn things around so she can emerge smiling, has always amazed me.

And anyone who knows this spirited woman knows that she has played all the roles in her life, from daughter and mother, to dancer, actress, philanthropist and seeker, with aplomb, using grit and determination to fulfil each role to the best of her ability.

This book brings all her varied selves together, and knits the story of her life through her constant seeking for wellness and good health, not only for herself, but for her family and the extended community that forms her dance-based organisation, Darpana.

With no bashfulness or coy sidestepping, Mallika talks about her mistakes, her misadventures with diets as an adolescent, her adventures into Ayurveda, naturopathy, homeopathy and even hypnotism. She shares the benefits that each brought to her life.

As someone steeped in wellness and aesthetic beauty myself, I believe she does a rare service to the cause of good health by revealing the blunders of her youth and sharing the lessons she learnt from them.

Many a young woman, or even a young man, may find lessons here and be able to sift away the confusing advice that floats about regarding weight control, skincare and allergies, and find clearcut advice on how to use exercise, yoga and food to keep healthy, supple and stay youthful.

In a world confused and beaten by a pandemic that proved us vulnerable beyond our own comprehension, Mallika offers a ray of tried and tested guidelines to a good life.

Of course the book is intensely personal, but that's how she has always been: colouring her dance and her writing with stories from her own experience.

Cheers to you, dear girl!

—Dr Jamuna Pai
Cosmetologist, Mumbai

Introduction

In Search of a Holistic Life

The advancement of a Western scientific allopathic system of medicine all over the world for the last seventy years has made an unbelievable contribution to disease control. The technological and surgical procedures and invention of new medications have contributed a lot to human healthcare and well-being but the rising number of lifestyle and chronic diseases is a major cause for alarm in healthcare management today.

In the last thirty-five years the best Western medical institutions around the world have been seeking better answers through traditional systems of medicine. Different systems of medicine like Ayurveda, with thousands of years of exposure to mankind, Chinese medicine, and Herbalism in Africa and South America, have a lot to offer in health management. The benefits of integrating different systems of medicine with or without Western medicine is the trend of the future among the medical fraternity. Integrative Medicine, as it is known, is the concept of incorporating different systems of medicine in treating a medical condition, improving health or prevention of disease. Post Covid, health promotion and improvement of the immune system is the need of the hour. This is not possible only with Western medicine but a holistic and integrative approach is the answer.

Medical universities around the world have started to integrate Western medicine with one or the other traditional system of medicine where yoga has got the maximum acceptance because of its benefits that have been proven through research findings.

My journey of integration started with incorporating yoga with homeopathic practice in Europe and the UK in the mid-1980s. My presentation at the 101 Clinic, London, on the benefits of integrating Western medicine with homeopathy, yoga, naturopathy, acupuncture, psychology, spiritual healing, diet and nutrition brought out a lot of benefits of this approach for chronic disease management.

Introduction

This search for knowledge made me travel to China to study acupuncture and Chinese medicine at the WHO Institute of Chinese Medicine, Nanjing.

In 1989, I organised the Holistic & Integrated Medicine Conference, bringing experts and practitioners from around the world to Bangalore (now Bengaluru), including HH Dalai Lama, Dr Andrew Weil and Swami Sachidananda, to speak on the importance of holistic and integrated medicine, including the role of spirituality in health and healing which India is known for.

The AYUSH systems of medicine (Ayurveda, Naturopathy, Unani, Siddha, Homeopathy) is official and very popular in India. We are lucky to have all these systems of medicine available in world-class institutions and research centres as well as in private and government hospitals. More and more people are seeking these natural systems of medicine and their popularity has increased manifold post the Covid pandemic.

Integrated medicine or healthcare is not another term for complementary medicine, nor does it represent an alternative to Western medicinal care. An integrated approach is much wider. It has a focus on health and healing, not just disease and treatment. An integrative and holistic approach is to treat a person as a whole (mind, body and spirit) by combining the ancient medical techniques, modern medical advancements and complementary therapies for true healing. The process of healing is planned by considering one's physiological, psychological, emotional, spiritual, nutritional, social and lifestyle factors rather than focussing only on the symptom or behaviour. The root cause of the symptom or behaviour is identified and accordingly the treatment plan is designed based on the individual.

The success of Integrative Medicine lies in the ability to select and blend the appropriate systems of medicine, without compromising on the authenticity of each individual system. Apart from having a full-fledged knowledge of each system, it is important for the holistic physician to have the wisdom and experience in implementing the integration of systems. When done appropriately, this combination enhances the healing powers of the various approaches. The selection and incorporation of appropriate complementary therapies that will not interfere with the systems of medicines that have been selected, is of utmost importance.

For example, in the case of an acute emergency asthmatic attack, allopathic inhalers or steroids may be used to control it but for long-term treatment Ayurvedic and homeopathic medicines could be very

Introduction

useful. It could be maintained by therapeutic yoga and breathing and supported by a naturopathic diet and lifestyle modification.

My experiments with integrating different systems of medicine along with Western medicine have yielded amazing results in the most complex medical conditions.

In my experience of thirty years, a good doctor will be holistic in nature irrespective of the system of medicine he or she practises. A patient may move from one system to another depending on the situation. Ultimately, several conditions that have proved to be non-curable by allopathic medicine may be completely cured by natural methodology. This is applicable to a large number of chronic diseases. The more I treat patients with this holistic approach, the more convinced I am that the future of medicine is the integration of different systems focussing on prevention, early intervention and cure.

I have known Mallika for more than twenty years and she is one of the most ardent followers of holistic health. She is a regular at Soukya, my holistic health centre in Bangalore—she was one of our earliest patients and continues to come every year for her 'retreat'.

Her deep understanding and belief in non-

Introduction

conventional integrative holistic medicines is explained very well in this book. Through talking about her own personal experiences and practical usage, she has given an insight into so-called 'inexplicable' healing techniques.

I would recommend this book to anybody who is seeking a better understanding of our ancient systems of healing and wants to benefit from them.

—Dr Issac Mathai
*Chairman and Director,
Soukya International Holistic Health Centre,
Bengaluru*

1

How It All Began

I was a plump child with a healthy appetite. I was also the younger of two siblings in my family and the youngest in an extended family of ten cousins. My cousins and my brother Kartikeya teased me mercilessly about what I ate, when I ate and what I ate it with. Rice, butter, sugar, potatoes. In whatever combination.

We were a nuclear family—my father, the space scientist, Vikram Sarabhai; my mother, the dancer, writer, philosopher, Mrinalini Sarabhai; my older brother Kartikeya, now an environmentalist and educator, and me. The Sarabhais were considered the first family of Ahmedabad. Closely linked to Mahatma Gandhi, Rabindranath Tagore, Bertrand

Russell and Sir C.V. Raman, amongst others, the family was renowned for its pioneering role in the arts, the sciences and education, and for being deeply committed to the idea of building a new India. My grandmothers on both sides were closely involved with the Independence movement. Two of my aunts from each side of the family, Mridula Sarabhai from my father's side, and Captain Lakshmi Sehgal of the Indian National Army, my mother's elder sister, had spent years in and out of British jails. The family was blind to differences in caste and creed, gender, religion and nationality—boys and girls were treated the same way and were brought up to be free thinkers of fierce independence. One aunt, Bharati, was part of the famed Bloomsbury group, avant-garde and non-conformist writers in London. On my mother's side, too, the Kerala women were fighters for justice and freedom, and tales about them abound in the region.

My Sarabhai grandparents, Ambalal and Sarladevi, had wanted their eight children, born between 1910 and 1922, to be trained for international lives, comfortable anywhere, although unequivocally Indian. This was reflected in many ways, through languages spoken in the house, twin sitting rooms, one Indian style, the other Western, and through food. Lunches were eaten in thalis, sitting Gujarati style on a patlo, eating with one's hands. Dinner was a different affair. Seated at a dining table and eating with the correct knives and spoons, vegetarian Western fare was served. The children could distinguish at a young age the correct spoons for soup and dessert!

In a slightly different fashion, the practice came into our home. While both meals were at the dining table and not on low seats, lunches were Indian, eaten with our hands. As ours was a mixed family, the food could be from anywhere in India, Tamil one day, Kathiawadi or Marwadi the next. Papa was a foodie and loved variety, but was also a health fiend, so fried food was not a frequent part of lunch. Dinners were non-Indian, usually Continental but also from Mexico or Indonesia.

By the time I was five years old, I had started going to school and lunch was had there. Awful overcooked vegetables of green, yellow, red. Ugh. I wanted white. Every day before leaving home, I would hide some sugar wrapped in paper in my shirt pocket. I would toss a handful over everything on my school thali and gulp it down, ending with a generous pinch of pure sugar, tossed into my mouth. It helped take away the taste of the vegatables! My favourite sandwich was white bread and butter with wedges of potato fries.

The other favourite was chocolate, solid or liquid. Milk chocolate. Chocolate milk.

IN FREE FALL

I used to go to my mother's dance classes because all my friends went. I would much rather have not. As a child, I was quite lazy, and would have much preferred to play carrom or cards or read a book. But all my friends went to Amma's classes and there was nobody to play with! So, yielding to early peer pressure, I joined the classes. I must have shown promise quite early because I was soon chosen for all the lead roles in the extravagant and complex performances at my school, Shreyas. But in general, till I was about sixteen and started playing badminton, I was a slow and unwilling participant in any sport or physical activity. I was the slowest runner in my team and everyone let out an exasperated sigh if I was in their relay team. I used to be quite good at shot-put, though. But my favourite sport was curling up on my bed with a book, or better, books. I could spend hours, days there. I was a very laid-back child. And a very shy one.

This suddenly changed when I hit puberty. Suddenly I wanted not to be plump. I wanted to be shapely, be able to wear what I wanted. I turned to my mother for advice. Amma was the wrong person to ask for tips on how to lose weight or get thin. She had little interest in food and a tiny appetite. She ate what is today considered all the wrong foods

and never put on an extra kilo. She had always been very thin. And she was fit enough to dance for many hours a day.

Papa, on the other hand, loved tasty and varied food but was also very conscious of being fit and slim and healthy. He woke up at 4 a.m. and drank four glasses of water before doing his Surya Namaskars and going for a jog around the garden. His lunch was always a big green salad, one roti and vegetables. He began talking to me about food and health and fitness, when, at the age of thirteen, I went to him for help. He explained that thinness was an external, but what was more important was what we ate, how good it was for us, how it made us feel and function. He introduced me to greens, both cooked and uncooked. He dressed salads wonderfully and coaxed me into developing a taste for them. He made me try fruits other than mangoes and strawberries. And he lead by example.

Slowly over the next few years I made myself develop a taste for vegetables, for salads, for raw food. I started walking straighter (after Amma asked me if I wanted to be a dancer or a duck!), giving up on sweets, forcing myself to like fruits. I started thinking of my body as a part of who I was. And thus started the long and often arduous journey that has lead me to where I am today.

How It All Began

I invite you to walk my path with me, for better or worse, up mountains and into ditches. And to make peace with your body, your mind, and with each and every muscle and muscle ache in it.

2

Every Diet Is Worth a Try

For many years I was only concerned with being thin. At a young age ill health seemed of no concern, and I assumed that I was and would stay healthy, no matter what diet I followed! The only drawback being that the food at home was delicious and varied, so while I had a lot to choose from, the temptations were also many.

When my parents married in 1942 and Amma came to live in the largely vegetarian state of Gujarat, she, a meat-eater all her life till then, was miserable. In the first two months she became even skinnier than she was, so much so that my father worried she had contracted some illness. Brought up on a combination of South Indian and Western food (she had Irish nannies and went to school in Switzerland), Amma started looking for vegetables that tasted vaguely like meat, and tried to find recipes for them. Amma started converting recipes from across the world into vegetarian avatars. By the time I was born a pattern had been set—Indian food for lunch and a lighter, non-Indian meal for dinner. This particularly suited my parents, both of whom continued working post dinner, Papa at his science laboratory and Amma back at Darpana, the academy she and Papa had set up for dance and the performing arts in 1949. Several decades before they became known to the new middle and upper classes in India, we were eating Vichyssoise soup, Burmese spaghetti, spring rolls and cheese soufflé at home.

At the age of fifteen, I got an Alliance Française scholarship to go and study French in Paris for a month. I went. Away from home and alone for the first time, I was miserable. After hopeless attempts at staying as a paying guest, I moved in with the family of Papa's counterpart in the French Atomic Energy Commission, Dr Goldschmidt, and his generous, loving wife, Naomi. Meat-eaters themselves, they had their cook make special delicacies for me. And missing home as I did, I compensated with food. Baguettes and cheese, quiches and lots and lots of desserts. Voila! A month later I had put on twenty pounds. This time I was seriously huge, the fattest I had ever been. In the college where my French classes were held, I was part of a gang called 'The Beauties', with Parveen Babi who went on to become a Bollywood star, and Kavita Bhambhani, a future Miss India (now the interior designer, Kavita Singh, actor Sonam Kapoor's aunt). I needed to lose weight, and quickly. I started playing badminton. I started running. I cut out all sweets and most meals. And slowly the pounds went.

My first serious body torture (self-inflicted, of course) started at the Indian Institute of Management back home in Ahmedabad. I was nineteen. The mess food was really bad but the evening tea shop on campus offered a good maska bun. I would have gorged on this if I could, but I thought I needed to lose weight. So I went on a self-developed Complan diet. It was simple, really. Tea with milk and saccharine at breakfast. One glass of Complan for lunch. Tea at teatime. Complan for dinner. Cigarettes whenever I got hungry. The sole exception was when huge tiffins arrived from home. My gang of four friends and I fell on it like we had never seen food before. Looking back, this diet of cigarettes and Complan could not have been good for me. Youthful exuberance and arrogance saw me through. The second phase of this was a slight variation, with an orange a day being added.

But I still felt the need to be thin. My next diet was a calorie-controlled one—900 calories, to be exact. I weighed every ounce of food, measured spoonfuls of liquids, counted calories, wrote everything down, sometimes splurged. I started avoiding rice and wheat, eating a lot of fruit and going on fruit fasts, only watermelon for a couple of days, or pineapple or grapefruit. I developed a liking for salads, if the dressing was right (Papa made the perfect Caesar salad dressing, with crisp crotons that didn't become limp, and lots of crushed garlic). I threw potatoes off my diet.

I forced myself to eat green vegetables like saag (spinach) and lauki (bottle gourd) by themselves, not as accompaniments to chapati or rice. I avoided dal. This became an on-and-off staple diet for many years. But I did have weekly binges, mostly rice and dosas. (The first money I ever earned or won was in a pani puri eating competition where I ate fifty-one puris. I was eleven. My competition was my childhood friend, the actor Anang Desai, of *Khichdi* fame).

All through this period, between the ages of sixteen and thirty, one of my main goalposts was to be thin. Today I look back at photographs and I see a slim girl, a slim woman. Except post the Paris trip, I *was* thin. Why then was I always trying to lose weight?

Anorexia setting in? Or a hangover from childhood, when I was constantly teased for how much I ate?

Then came the Atkins diet. The year was 1972 and Dr Robert Atkins propounded something revolutionary in his diet and best-selling book. Instead of calorie counting, which basically made one reduce fats and high-calorie proteins, this diet suggested eating fats and proteins and reducing carbohydrates. A challenge for an eggetarian. No carbs? A diet of eggs, cream, butter and cheese? For the first two days, I thought I was in heaven. After the third day I was longing for crunchy greens. For texture. For colour. But I plodded along. To check on ketosis, the fat-burning process, I peed on a sliver of paper that changed colour if ketosis was in progress. I would steal a green bean from Amma's plate at dinner, and then be tormented by guilt till the next morning's pee assured me that I was still in ketosis. By the end of the week my sweat started smelling bad. My mouth had a lousy taste. My hair started falling. I didn't feel good. I couldn't bear looking at eggs. Though I cheated many a time, I would force myself to get back on the diet until eventually I gave up.

Years later I read that Atkins died of too much of his own diet. Or so it was believed. The diet was demonized for decades as saturated fat was thought to lead to blocked arteries and heart attacks. Today, over twenty long-term studies have been done on the effect of this diet on the body and it seems to have gained respectability again. The studies seem to prove that saturated fats are harmless and the diet, in fact, leads to the promotion of HDL, the 'good' cholesterol. Many other diets have been born as variations of the original Atkins diet. However, I still feel that while it may be effective in quick weight loss, leaving out fruits and vegetables for extended periods cannot be good for one.

Then there was the Threptin version of the Complan diet where I replaced meals with four Threptin biscuits. Threptin biscuits are protein biscuits and used to be promoted for athletes and growing children. Today they come with recipes, rather like the nutri-nugget soya protein, but in my youth these had not been developed. I just ate four biscuits and drank down a couple of glasses of water for lunch and dinner. I have to admit, tastewise, Complan won.

And of course, I tried readymade meal replacements. Papa had always had a tendency to put on weight, and controlled it and his love of new and different food through sheer discipline. Once, whilst on a trip to teach at Harvard University in the US, he came upon a diet replacement food called Metrical. Each sachet had to be mixed with water and turned into a glass of 'milkshake' that replaced a meal. There were several flavours. Strawberry, vanilla and chocolate are the ones I recall clearly—I must have been about eleven at the time. Whilst on the trip he tried it and lost weight. Papa was then CEO of Sarabhai Chemicals, our pharmaceutical company, and decided to collaborate with the makers of Metrical to produce an Indian version. Limical was born. He brought it home in triumph for all of us who were willing to try it. It was supposed to be chilled and shaken in a mixer and served like a milkshake. Except it tasted bad. I desperately tried to like one of the flavours enough to be able to try it out for a couple of weeks, but failed. It used to make me want to retch. Despite huge marketing efforts, and Papa's high recommendations, the product did not succeed in the Indian market. Or at our home.

At some stage I started reading about macrobiotics and the Japanese lifestyle. It fascinated me. It is believed that during the Edo period in Japan, poor people were not allowed to eat meat and their food consisted of rice and soya products. Over decades it was seen that they lived longer and were healthier and the eating pattern was adopted by others. While some experts consider it a fad, even today the Japanese eat primarily a macrobiotic diet consisting of fish, nuts, beans, seeds, soya and its products and seaweed of different kinds. Considering that even today Japan has some of the oldest healthy people in the world, with centenarians not at all uncommon, this seemed to make sense.

I decided to try out the brown rice diet, for rice was and remains a favourite food. This falls within the macrobiotic theories but is more specific, and as I find rice very satisfying, it seemed a possible fit. I stocked up on Kerala rice and had it cooked and served in a Japanese bowl with sautéed vegetables, different ones every day. To add to the mood, I ate this with chopsticks. Rice for breakfast, lunch and dinner. For a while it was very enjoyable and after many years I could eat rice guilt-free. But having the same food day in and day out is tedious, even if it starts off as your favourite food. I yearned for a diversity of textures and tastes and look and feel. So I said goodbye to this one.

About thirty-five years ago I read about the Rotation Diet. What intrigued me was that it used the body's systems, the brain and the digestive system, to trick itself into losing weight. I read that our brain still retains its 'feast or fast' responses that we needed in primordial times. In early times when humans were hunter-gatherers, food availability was not a certainty. Sometimes a group would find a big animal and there would be plenty of food for many days. They would feast. Then for days they may find nothing, and they would get by on very little, or perhaps nothing but water. They would fast. The brain, research shows us, takes forty-eight hours to realise that it needs to shift from fast to feast or vice versa, to boost the metabolic system if more food needs to be digested, or to slow down the use of calories as fuel, if there is little to eat. It is this feature of the brain that the Rotation Diet uses.

One cycle of the diet lasts for three weeks. Weeks 1 and 3 are the same. On days 1, 2 and 3 women are allowed 600 and men 900 calories. On the next four days this goes up to 900 for women and 1200 for men. Week 2 is 1200 calories per day for women and 1500 for men. This is feast time. Week 3 follows the same pattern as Week 1. The fourth week is maintenance week with women sticking to 1200 calories and men to 1500. Activity levels also increase every week, going from half an hour of daily exercise for the first week to 45 minutes and then to 60 minutes in Week 3. In addition, we are allowed to choose one fruit for the duration, and are allowed three portions of the fruit per day, without counting them into our daily allowance. I found an apple the most satisfying but rarely needed more than one a day.

Keeping a food diary and a food weighing machine are crucial. The first three days are hard and just sometimes, I needed to resort to all three portions of fruit. But the most amazing thing about this diet is that as long as you keep within the calorie count you can eat anything. Sometimes, if I had a craving for something 'bad' like dal vadas, I just ate that and avoided other food to keep within the calorie limit. That meant that I could have all 600 calories in one 'bad' food and nothing the rest of the day. Likewise, a piece of cake worth 600 calories could be bitten into, through the day! And Week 2 really seemed like a feast. I often ended up with calories to spare at the end of the day but that is not allowed either. So I would eat a small piece of cheese (my favourite) or take another helping of something.

The other great thing about the diet is that it works. Extremely effectively. I used to keep repeating cycles continuously or once every three or four months and I never got bored.

By this time health was as big a concern for me as being thin, and this diet allowed me to eat from all food groups and eat very healthy.

Here is a typical cycle for me:

Breakfast: Half a grapefruit, one thin slice wholewheat toast and a slice of a hard cheese.

Or

Half a banana, one cup oats with skim milk or a slice of wholewheat bread and peanut butter and an apple.

Lunch: Four oz of paneer, sautéed or grilled, a big bowl of 500 gms of cooked spinach.

Dinner: 500 gms sautéed cauliflower, or cabbage or mushrooms, and two small pieces of wholewheat toast, or chapatis without ghee.

For the 900- and 1200-calorie weeks, I added measured amounts of what I really missed—a slice of cheese, more toast, a soup, a dal. What is important is to keep the calorie count correct, and the day nutritious.

Many years later, about seven years ago, I met Rujuta Diwekar. By then I had long been a convert to holistic healing and a holistic world view. I still had a niggling issue with being a couple of kilos more than the weight I found best for dancing and looking the way I wanted. I had read her book, *Don't Lose Your Mind, Lose Your Weight*,[*] and everything she said made absolute sense and was totally up my street. After the

---

[*] First published Random House India, 2009; reprinted Penguin Random House, Ebury Press, 2019.

consultation I switched to her frequent eating plan and that too worked for me. It gave a space for cravings and for huge variety. She had convenient options for when I was travelling or in a conference or whatever situation that my lifestyle put up as 'problems', reasons to go off the eating pattern. While I don't follow it meticulously anymore, I am naturally someone who can't eat much at a single meal and get hungry at non-meal times, so her frequent small meals is what I do. And I eat ghee every day to keep my insides lubricated.

Over the years, however, I have seen and know what my body does, when it does it and when I need to clean up my act. Today I give myself leeway to eat and drink what I feel like if I am travelling, to enjoy my food and wine, to allow myself luxuries, to sometimes even miss yoga or dance practice. Because I know when I must get back to my normal again. Fitness and healthwise.

3

Inside Outside

I really love food. The variety, the textures, the tastes, the delicacies, the nuances. And I love trying new foods from different lands which have their own, individualistic palletes of herbs and spices. So in the years before I had found my equilibrium as far as food and health went, before I was even concerned with health, in my carefree mid-twenties, it was hard to be constantly wanting to be thin and constantly travelling and wanting to taste new tastes.

That was over four decades ago. Anorexia and bulimia had not found their way into our consciousness. These were not even names we knew, let alone the unhealthy head space that led to them.

For the uninitiated: *Anorexia nervosa* is an eating disorder that causes people to obsess about weight and what they eat. It is characterized by a distorted body image with an unwarranted fear of being overweight. People with anorexia will go to extreme lengths to stay thin and prevent weight gain, including severely restricting their calorie intake, skipping meals, fasting and even starvation. Some of the side effects of anorexia are extreme weight loss and thinness, low blood counts, fatigue, insomnia, dizziness or fainting spells, hair that thins, breaks or falls out, and even a disruption of the menstrual cycle.*

Bulimia, on the other hand, is an eating disorder characterized by binge eating followed by purging. According to the *Mayo Family Health Book*, bulimia is a serious, potentially life-threatening eating disorder. People with bulimia may secretly binge—eating large amounts of food with a loss of control over the eating—and then purge, trying to get rid of the extra calories in an unhealthy way such as self-induced vomiting or misuse of laxatives, weight-loss supplements, diuretics or enemas after bingeing. Or they may use other ways to get rid of extra calories and prevent weight gain, such as fasting, strict dieting

---

* *Mayo Clinic Family Health Book*, 5th edition.

or excessive exercise. Like people with anorexia, those who have bulimia are preoccupied with weight and body shape and usually have unrealistic expectations of what their 'ideal' body should be. Because it is related to self-image, and not just about food, bulimia can be hard to overcome.

In my early twenties I was deeply in love with a man from Kenya. I travelled to Kenya to see the country for myself, and to explore whether he was the man I wanted to marry. As his own home was in the process of being renovated, I stayed at the home of close friends of his family. The lady of the house, a sharp businesswoman, ran a kitchen that produced delicious vegetarian cuisine. At every meal I used to watch her gorge on food and then quietly disappear for about ten minutes. She would return with slightly red eyes but fresh lipstick, looking relaxed and cheerful as though nothing was amiss. The same at the next meal. And the next.

For the first few days I was too polite to ask what was happening. Then as we became closer and she started, in some senses, mentoring me about life amongst the expats in Africa, she asked me if I didn't like the food in her home. I loved it, I said. 'Then why do you eat so little?' she asked. I told her that I was terrified of putting on weight. 'Oh, then just do what I do. Eat as much as you like and then stick your fingers down your throat. All pleasure and no guilt or worry.'

It took me a few days to get my head around the thought and not be revulsed by it. Then one afternoon I decided to try it. I ate plentifully and drank a lot of water with my meal. And then rushed off to one of the bathrooms. As soon as I put my fingers into my mouth, I gagged and my stomach heaved but nothing else happened. After two or three unsuccessful attempts, I came out crestfallen and with a very sore throat that did not allow the next trial for a few days.

I could have given up, but the thought of eating what I liked, as much as I liked, when I liked (as long as a clean loo was around) was too tempting. At the end of two weeks I had become a pro.

Ah, the pleasures of eating without the fear of gaining weight. For someone who had been on one diet or another for over a decade, this was freedom and bliss indeed. And as I went further down this path, I started developing techniques to make the throwing up faster and more effective, finding muscles in my stomach that could push the food up more quickly.

There was, however, one problem that I never managed to solve and that got me into really embarrassing situations in the years that followed.

Inside Outside

My vomiting was loud, and try as I did, there was nothing I could do about it. In restaurants where there were individual loos with thick doors, it was fine. But in most homes where I was invited to dine, the loo for guests was just off the sitting or dining area, and alas, never soundproof. Many have been the awful occasions when I have come back to the table to quizzical, sometimes pitying looks, and deadly silence. I always mumbled something about suddenly having a stomach upset, an excuse that must have irritated my hostesses, who often went to great lengths to make special vegetarian food for me, no end.

This way of keeping thin was so easy that it became something I did after every meal regardless of whether I was eating at a restaurant or someone's home, or travelling. I would eat a decent breakfast and keep that in. But the minute I thought I had overeaten, it was as though I couldn't keep the food down. I had to get it out. And this meant every day at home as well, to the disgust, and then worry of my family. My brother named it the 'inside outside technique'—several years before I became the publisher of the magazine of the same name.

I finally stopped this absurd behaviour only in 2001, after several of the cringeworthy dinner episodes mentioned above, happened in New York high society

and I was at risk of being declared *persona non grata* in many homes!

I look at photographs of mine from that period. I am skinny. What went on in my mind? I was definitely suffering from both bulimia and anorexia! Thankfully, it happened years before it had become a psychological phenomenon to be treated by therapists. And thankfully I got out of it without, I think, too much damage to my health—both mental and physical.

My Kenyan engagement ended badly, with my breaking it when I realised that my life would be run by my mother-in-law. As mentioned in another chapter, this lead to a long depression and then to my finding dance. But the 'inside outside' went on for another two decades after this.

4

The Smoking Gun and Other Addictions

No one in my immediate family had ever smoked. I was never attracted to it either, although several of my older buddies smoked. I was not even interested in taking a drag, as we called it, just to feel more sophisticated. And then I got admission to the Indian Institute of Management, Ahmedabad. I had just turned nineteen.

At the IIM, work was assigned to groups of students rather than on a one-on-one basis. There were only nine girls in a class of 200, so each of us was in an all-male group, usually with ten or twelve boys. We would be cooped up in a room for many hours of the night, for many nights on end. And except for me and perhaps one or two others, everyone in the groups chain-smoked.

I had long lustrous hair that was almost knee-length. Each morning after these sessions, not only my clothes, but my hair would reek of cigarettes. At first I felt revolted, but slowly, unfortunately, I started enjoying the smell. From there to the first experimental drag on someone's cigarette was just a step away. Within a few months I was hooked.

My cigarette of choice was Benson & Hedges, difficult to find in Ahmedabad. I had to use a lot of planning and cunning to ensure a steady supply of cartons from Bombay.

My smoking was never hidden from my family, and although they hated it, I smoked openly at home and wherever I was. Amma wrinkled her nose in distaste when I would smoke, dressed in full Bharatanatyam regalia. But the awful health effects of smoking were not well known then, so no one was panicking.

By the late 1970s I was smoking forty cigarettes a day and had graduated to Dunhill, a stylish Dunhill lighter always accompanying me. I periodically thought of quitting; quit, and immediately put on weight. Smoking definitely cut down hunger pangs and became a part of my 'stay thin' regime. 'Do I want to live fat or die thin?' was the idiotic question I used to ask myself. The answer was, of course, 'I want to be thin.' Over the next many years I tried to quit many times over, somewhat half-heartedly. By now the link between smoking and cancer had been well established. I also knew that for pregnant women smoking was dangerous and could injure the child. I consoled myself by saying that if I ever wanted a child, I would quit a year before getting pregnant.

I had developed a funny quirk that accompanied my smoking. I had to have a piece of sweet supari in my mouth. Without this, half the pleasure of the cigarette was lost. Many years earlier Amma had given me a lovely brass paandaan, the size of my palm, and this became my permanent supari box, always replenished, always in my handbag, travelling the world with me.

In 1982, in New York, I met a man who I knew I wanted to marry and have a child with. I was clear about quitting smoking now. But how? I was on top of my career as a dancer, slim and svelte with no effects of smoking on my lungs. How could I avoid the inevitable weight gain?

Ruth Schwartz, then vice president of Macy's Inc., the huge department store company, was a friend, and she suggested I visit a hypnotist called Dr Nathan

Fleischer. 'He specialises in smoking and weight loss,' she told me. 'He is booked for months but I have a close friend who can get us an appointment.'

On the 7th of May, 1982, at 11.30 in the morning, I got an appointment with the good doctor. He had a clinic on the posh Fifth Avenue, way downtown, on 11th Street. In my handbag I had two fresh packets of Dunhill, then very difficult to find in the US. I waited in the doctor's outer office, somewhat nervous and not very optimistic. His assistant came out and asked me to fill a form. I filled it and handed it back. 'Two hundred dollars, please,' she said, stretching out a hand. Wow, that was steep. I handed it to her and was asked to wait.

Dr Fleischer looked very old and grizzled. He was bent, with a decided hump. 'So, I am told that you are a dancer and an actress. Then this should be easy for you. It's all about imagining things. And you must have a powerful imagination, to be an artist.'

He then asked me to open my bag. I did so, grudgingly. Two packets of Dunhill fell out. He took them, threw them on the floor and jumped on them several times. My heart sank. My thrifty Gujarati self also thought of how many dollars that was worth—British, imported cigarettes were very expensive in those days, besides being difficult to find. 'You won't need those anymore,' he said, smiling cherubically. I grimaced inwardly.

He asked me to relax on the chaise longue. 'I am going to count down from five. By the time I come to one, you will be completely hypnotised,' he said to me. Fat chance, I said to myself. I shut my eyes. His voice changed to a soft and dreamy one. He started counting down. My thoughts continued to be sceptical, disbelieving that anyone could go under so easily. My mind was still racing as he said, 'Now you are completely in my control. I want you to imagine a hill and meadows, and a lovely breeze. Now imagine you are running up the hill. Your lungs are clear. Now you are not huffing and out of breath. You are energetic. Your lungs fill with oxygen. Run and enjoy it.' I am listening. I am awake. I am scoffing at what he is saying. Smoking has not yet had the effect of making me breathless. I can run up a hill without huffing and puffing. My lungs are clear. This is nonsense. What a waste of my packets of cigarettes and two hundred dollars. I could have done so much with that amount of money!

Meanwhile the good doctor was still speaking to me. Now he asked me to imagine a mouth with cancer, the awful holes, the pain, the agony, the inability to open it. I imagined all of this, saying to myself, 'You

are an actress, Mallika. All you are doing is acting as though you are hypnotised.'

And then I heard him say, 'I am going to once again count down from five to one. When I say one, you will be fully awake.' Yeah, big deal, I thought. I have not been asleep, so how can I awaken!

He counted down. I opened my eyes, pretending to have been deep in a hypnotic state. I stood up. He picked up a card up from his desk and handed it to me. 'I am in Miami and LA every week. This card has all my numbers. If you feel like lighting up, call me collect. Any time.' And he showed me out.

I was early for a lunch date with my prospective husband so I decided to walk uptown instead of taking a subway. And as I walked my eyes searched for a cigarette shop that may sell Dunhill. I waited for the urge. It did not come. Not then, not since. It is forty years since this encounter. I have felt no urge to smoke. Nor did I feel the need to overeat to compensate for not smoking, as I had so many times earlier. Yes, for the first week or so, my fingers felt lost not holding a cigarette, as did my lips. And my supari box remained full. But that is all.

Nearly four decades. And I still don't believe I was hypnotised.

I was a light party drinker for years. But I drank only wine, I hated the taste of any other liquor.

Things changed in 1984, when I moved to Paris for two years, and then travelled across the world until 1990, performing in the international production of Peter Brook's *The Mahabharata*. In Paris, to drink wine with meals or in cafés, was the normal thing to do. If one hung out with friends, or dined out, or met buddies, it was good wine that one drank. And as a cheese fanatic, red wine was the perfect drink. But hard liquor was something I still eschewed.

Over the five years that I spent playing Draupadi in *The Mahabharata*, I continued drinking and enjoying wine, and in Japan, at the end of the tour, saké. By now a glass of wine had become a bottle of wine at a meal. I enjoyed the taste, and I enjoyed the effect. And back in India, where the wine market was practically non-existent in the early '90s, I missed it.

My mother strongly disapproved of drinking. She had been brought up in a very Victorian household in Madras (now Chennai), and she saw it as something wrong and sinful. But when Papa died from what was believed to be a sudden cardiac arrest at the age of fifty-one in December 1971, she struggled with insomnia and grief. Instead of giving her a sleeping pill, her doctor suggested she have a drink. She baulked at this and wouldn't even consider it for many months. But she was getting worn out with grief and we persuaded her to try it. Finally she agreed and we started giving her a glass of whisky each evening. She hated the taste in the beginning, but from the first night on, seemed more relaxed. And she slept better. Slowly this became a ritual, shared with one or other of her friends who would drop by, and she started looking forward to those couple of hours, spent watching tennis and cricket on TV, and chatting with the friend, before dinner.

I started joining her when I wasn't travelling, which wasn't often. My career was flying high and I was often on long two- and three-month tours abroad, or shuttling in and out of Ahmedabad on overnight jaunts to different parts of India. And when I travelled, every evening I was somewhere where everyone drank.

When did I start depending on alcohol, to lose myself, to allow it to be what destressed me, to allow me to lock out the world? I think it was in 2002, when I took on the government and started being hounded and hunted.

The Gujarat pogrom had just happened. Well-orchestrated crowds of Hindus, armed with petrol to burn and trishuls to maim and behead, roamed the streets of Ahmedabad and Gujarat raping, killing, burning Muslims. As is happening in so many parts of India today, the police and the authorities stood by and watched, even aided the vicious mobs. Neighbours turned on neighbours, families on loyal retainers. It was a carnage. Over 2,200 Muslims were killed, hundreds of women raped and hundreds of thousands made homeless.

This blatant misuse of power by the machinery that is supposed to follow the Constitution to safeguard India's people, appalled me. I felt I could not remain silent at this huge breach of our rights as citizens. With two colleagues I filed a petition in the Supreme Court against the administration and the police, holding them responsible for the carnage. We were pitting ourselves against the state government and all its administrative wings, the police included. What followed was a long legal battle, the filing of many other cases, cases being clubbed together, the involvement of the National Human Rights Commission, the setting aside of some of the cases to be dealt with in other states, the involvement of bodies like Human Rights Watch, and, in the long run, the general steamrolling and whitewashing of facts.

The reprisal by the state was swift and hard. I had a series of cases filed against me, some as absurd as the cook in the Darpana Café accusing me of stealing pots and pans, to the very serious one of promoting illegal immigration in the guise of dance tours. My passport was impounded. I had to report to the local police station twice a day, every day for months. Every attempt was made to break me and Darpana over the next many years, with threats to my children and family, arrest warrants, intimidation, economic pauperisation of Darpana and much, much more. In the eyes of the government, I remain a pariah even today.

I believe that is when my dependence on the evening drink started. Let me not kid myself by saying that I did not enjoy it. I did. I loved the taste of good alcohol. And, like my mother, it made sleep at night possible.

Over the years the dependence grew stronger. I would start looking forward to that hour of the day when I could have my first drink. And although I was plagued by guilt, I could not stop. As with my cigarette addiction, because of all the other positive things I did regularly for my body, from vitamins to yoga to good eating and plenty of water and exercise, the effect of this abuse of my body didn't manifest itself in ways in which it could have without that safety net, and so there was no health crisis that would compel me to stop.

Once again, I turned to hypnosis. This time, it didn't work. I have tried homeopathy. I have tried abstinence. Whenever possible I have tried sticking only to wine and cutting out the hard stuff. For the two weeks, twice a year, when I am having my panchakarma treatments, I cleanse. Periodically, I go on cleansing fasts.

But I remain a work in progress.

5
Finding Dance and Yoga

I first started learning yoga at the Kaivalyadhama Yoga Institute in Bombay (now Mumbai) in 1974 while spending a year there trying to figure out if I wanted a life as a film actress. Kaivalyadhama was founded in Lonavala in the late 1920s to disseminate the yoga teaching of Swami Kuvalayanandaji. Swamiji had been doing extensive research into yoga and modern science and was teaching these methods for health and healing. Soon it became apparent that more and more of the people who wanted to learn were coming from Bombay. They persuaded Swamiji to set up a branch in Bombay and this came into being in 1932. In the 1970s, this was *the* place to go to learn yoga.

Finding Dance and Yoga

At Shreyas, my school in Ahmedabad, we were taught all about holistic living, but somehow, yoga was never part of it. Papa used to do asanas at 5 a.m., an ungodly hour for me, so I was rarely privy to them; Amma, never. So I was not really exposed to yoga, growing up.

In Bombay I was getting bored and restless listening to endless useless 'starry' film scripts and needed to find a more worthwhile occupation. By this time my interest in wellness and being fit had taken root, and I felt I wanted and needed something that engaged my body. Yoga had intrigued me and I felt this was a good opportunity and time. So I enrolled myself at Kaivalyadhama. The few months of learning were great fun and I looked forward to getting to the institute every morning. Once back in Ahmedabad and while I was doing my PhD, I used to dance a little and do some asanas in my room, but I wasn't really committed to either dance or yoga, back then.

In 1976 I broke up with the man from Kenya whom I was engaged to. I was heartbroken, even though the decision to end the relationship had been entirely mine (and oh, so correct). I went into a deep depression and more or less locked myself up in my bedroom. I felt let down again, once by Papa and death, now by a man I loved and trusted and whom I did not expect would yield to a domineering mother. I could not stop telling myself that I could never trust men—a feeling I still battle with constantly, even twenty years into a very rich and committed relationship.

Our home, Chidambaram, in Ahmedabad, is on the banks of the Sabarmati (actually, used to be. Now the Sabarmati Riverfront project has taken the river further away and a highway borders us!). My bedroom had a glass-windowed wall facing our lawns and the river. My favourite chair is a large one with armrests that take a notebook or a computer and a seat that is wide enough to meditate cross-legged in. It was handed down from my great-aunt Anasuya Sarabhai, friend and colleague of Mahatma Gandhi, the woman who fought for labour rights in 1918 and founded the first labour union in India, to Papa and then to me. I spent four months of nothingness sitting in this chair, with my legs propped up on the windowsill, looking at the river and asking, why? Why did Papa die? Why did this man let me down?

And then, in a Eureka moment, I woke up one morning with a single thought: 'All I want is to dance.'

Amma had never tried to persuade me to take on dance as a career. Clever Amma. So finding it through a flurry of grief and grieving was a boon to both me and her. She too had felt lost after Papa's death. Even dance had begun to seem pointless. But having me commit to it was a second innings for her and we plunged ourselves into working together. I started relearning the rare dance pieces of Kuchipudi that my amazing guru, C.R. Acharyulu, had taught me, and that is when I found I needed to get back to regular yoga. The many sculpturesque poses that form the backbone of Kuchipudi demand a very flexible body and spine, and I found nothing better than asanas for this.

C.R. Acharyulu was a shishiya (disciple) of the guru credited with transforming the dance drama form of Bhagavata Mela Natakam into the solo Kuchipudi that we know today. This guru, Lakshminarayan Shastri, had two favourite students, my Master and the much more famed Vempati Chinna Satyam. Master arrived at Darpana in 1953, sent by Amma's friend, the art connoisseur S.V. Venugopal (then officially working for Lux soaps). Amma had set up Darpana some five years earlier and was looking for traditional gurus. Venugopal thought that Master, who also had a deep knowledge of the Shastras and of Andhra shadow puppets, would be a good fit. Master was invited to join Darpana and arrived from Elluru by train, a journey broken by many stops and many telegrams to Amma that read, 'Arrived xx. Taking rest. Will be newly arrived soon.' His English was amazing in its ability to evoke the right images through the most bizarre usage of words. Including always calling Amma 'Sir'. I inherited him at Darpana and started learning from him at the age of fifteen. He was one of my main sources of knowledge about our myths and legends, Shastras and texts. His joy in dance was perhaps what infected my Kuchipudi style the most.

Many years later, in 1999, I decided to introduce a yoga class for all the performers at Darpana, not only for flexibility, but also as a pooling into the common consciousness every morning that I felt was required in a performance company to work closely and creatively as a team. We have been doing this five days a week since then. And on tour wherever we are, as much as we can.

My yoga practice has changed from one that limbers up the muscles and makes the spine more flexible, to one that promotes wholeness and wellness and now, more recently, rehabilitates worn and torn muscles. Till recently we have always had teachers trained at the Shivananda Ashram in Ahmedabad. Then five years ago, having heard and read a lot about Iyengar yoga, I invited a teacher to come and take a two-week workshop. I was surprised that while there were Iyengar yoga classes in Budapest and Melbourne, there were none in Ahmedabad. The lovely Aarti Mehta, trained with her siblings by Guruji Iyengar himself, came to teach the workshop. She, her sister Rajvi and brother Birju have been running the main Iyengar Centres in Mumbai for years and are brilliant teachers. I loved what this type of yoga did and its possibilities for healing the body with props. Since then, we have had many Iyengar yoga workshops and they have now started online classes for Ahmedabad students as well. Jyoti Patel from the Shivananda Ashram has been teaching us at Darpana, and we alternate between Iyengar and Shivananda styles, sometimes doing asanas fast in what is called power yoga. Through the lockdown and the time after, when often my dance practice does not happen, and through a period of rehabilitation post an illness, it is my one hour of yoga that gives me the power to face each day, physically and mentally. On the weekends my body really misses it. Yes, I could do my asanas without a class, but doing it in a group has many positives, and a special energy.

Dance has become my go-to place for all moods and emotions—to celebrate, to weep, to vent anger and frustration, to feel alive, to feel strong, both emotionally and physically. And I don't necessarily mean Bharatanatyam and Kuchipudi. Often I play music loudly in my room and just dance as though I was at a party or a discotheque. I love learning folk dancing at our folk and tribal dance centre, Janavak, founded in 1980. In the early days we invited a family from a tribal community, a different one each time, to come and work with us for a month, learning not only their dance and music, but their lore, why they did things the way they did, why they believed in certain things, what their customs and colours meant. I remember inviting the family of the now famous Kalbelia dancer, Gulabo, in 1986. Both Gulabo and I had two-year-olds. We heard stories from her mother-in-law, and learned from her. I still love doing the Kalbelia dance. My personal repertoire goes from dances of the Gonds and Ao Nagas, to Bihu, Sambalpuri, Purulia Chhau and more. And Flamenco, which I learned for three months in New York, while I performed in *The Mahabharata*. Each style does something different to the mind and the body. Some are mystical and slow. Others vibrant. Others make your adrenalin pump and still others are aerobic and beautiful. Each invigorates differently. Each affects the mood differently.

Today science has proved repeatedly that dance unleashes oxytocin, serotonin and other 'feel good' chemicals in the body. Even if one doesn't feel like dancing, the physical act of it, with music, makes you release those chemicals and you do feel better, happier, more upbeat.

(Note: See the Appendix for the asanas we do every week at Darpana).

6

The Empty Sella

In 1976 I was offered a Gujarati film that I couldn't refuse, *Mena Gurjari*. This was a story that had been spoken about as the greatest tale in Gujarati by Kailash Pandya, head of the Darpana drama department, and my mother for years, and I had heard many stories of the stage production of it with Kailashbhai and the very well-known actress Dina Pathak in the lead roles. So when I was approached to do the title role I couldn't refuse. It had a good unit, led by Dinesh Rawal and the scriptwriter Ramsinhbhai Rathod, and my co-star Rajiv was nice enough. I enjoyed the shooting at Lakshmi Studios in Vadodara and on location at Pavagadh. The film ran to full houses for fifty-two weeks. I still have people breaking into its famous garba, Sathiya Puravo Dware, when they see me!

Mena Gurjari's huge box office success lead to a reblossoming of the Gujarati film industry, and offers began pouring in. Over the next few years I did many films, mostly bad ones. But the industry was gentle and a welcome change from the cut-throat and vulgar industry of commercial Hindi films that I had tried and left just after I graduated from the IIM in 1974.

One morning, about two years later, I woke up feeling odd, as though something had changed in my body. I went to the bathroom and stood over the sink still wondering what felt different. My eyes fell on the mirror and I was stunned. My face had swollen to nearly twice its size, my eyes disappearing into slits. I ran to Amma, half weeping. Amma calmed me down and spoke to the family doctor who suggested that it might be an allergic reaction that had led to edema. He made me take a diuretic and over the next few hours the swelling went down. A few days later it was back with a vengeance, this time with my fingers and toes also very swollen.

Over the next two months my body seemed to be falling apart. My periods stopped. My hair, luxurious and knee-length, started falling out. My weight was going up in leaps and bounds even though I reduced my food intake to one orange a day and one glass of Complan for each meal once again. I was panicked. For the first time I had no control over my body. It was doing strange things, making me look like a frog one day and a chimp the next and there was nothing I could do. Amma sent me to Madras, to meet my grandmother's (Ammaji) physician, Dr Cherian. He was head of the Railway Hospital and a wonderful person. After some preliminary tests he suggested that I had a thyroid imbalance, and put me on a course of thyroxine. I came back home. I was shooting frequently, and depending on how I looked, would often end up having to cancel shoots. I was desperate.

Things didn't improve with time. We needed wise counsel and there was no one to turn to. If only Papa were still with us. Amma turned to her dear friend, Jamshed Bhabha, worldly-wise and with the clout of the Tata family and industries behind him. Through friends at the Tata Hospital and his contacts abroad, he found out that the world's leading endocrinologist was Professor Victor Wynn at London's St Mary's Hospital. He managed to get in touch and fix an appointment for me in April. Amma and I would need to fly to London and stay there while I went through the tests. But where was the money going to come from?

Since Papa's death in 1971, the war between his older brother Gautam and us had come into the open and we had little access to our wealth. Times were hard financially, and we worried constantly about how to pay the bills. And now we needed at least Rs 1 lakh.

By this time I was getting a lot of Gujarati film offers, mostly rubbish that I turned down, though I was offered Rs 35,000 per film. (This may seem like a paltry amount by today's standards, but in the 1970s, in the regional film industry, it was not.) Now, in order to raise the money for the trip, I decided to take on whatever I was offered, and ended up doing four films in quick succession. I cringe to think of them now!

Ashok Advani, the lawyer and founder of the Businesss India group of magazines, had been a close friend for several years. He stepped in to help us out in the tough situation we were in. He flew to London and rented a place at Water Gardens, near Edgeware Road, and invited us stay with him as we went through the first gruelling days of tests. In the day and age when CAT scans and MRIs didn't exist, and when the science of endocrinology itself was very young, the testing was long and convoluted.

Professor Wynn was about as dour as the word allows. In all my time with him I never saw him

smile once. He looked at my papers and set me up for tests. He insisted that I stay at the hospital so that they could monitor my intake and output—he didn't believe me when I told him how little I ate and still put on weight. As I was not on social security or the National Health Service, being hospitalised would have been enormously expensive, so with great difficulty we convinced him that for the week that he wanted me monitored, I would stay as a day patient and ensure that I measured every sip of water I drank outside the hospital—eating was of course out of the question. Wynn had an assistant, a Yugoslavian woman, who was as charming as he was dour, who finally persuaded him. She remained a great comfort through the trying times that followed.

The nurses at St Mary's were very racist. The Prince of Oman, an enormous man with little English, was also being monitored alongside me. The nurses assumed that my English too must be poor and constantly muttered under their breath about how 'these foreigners' were taking advantage of their health system. Finally, after three days of awful food, boredom and nastiness, I put on my best British accent and told them in no uncertain terms how we were helping their economy, otherwise floundering, by bringing in foreign exchange They listened to me dumbfounded.

Their attitude suddenly changed, and they stopped being racist, at least with me. The Prince of Oman stayed on after I left and I don't know what his fate may have been.

By the end of a week of constant measuring of input and output, Wynn accepted that there was something amiss. I went through a cross-sectional X-ray of the brain and head called the multi-plenograph. And finally Amma was called into Wynn's office and told that I had a brain tumour, a pituitary tumour. I would need an immediate operation and he was consulting with others to decide whether to cut me open from the hairline down or from the nose up! (The pituitary is a pea-sized endocrine gland at the base of the brain, behind the bridge of the nose and directly below the hypothalamus. It is called the master gland of the endocrine system because it controls many other hormone glands in the body.)

Amma and I freaked out. Who could we turn to? Whom could we rely on to advise? There was no one. Papa had so much medical knowledge, and involved as he used to be in pharmaceuticals, would have called doctors across the world for second and third opinions. We felt at a loss. How could we suddenly plunge into brain surgery? And where would we find the money for it? Where would we stay?

B.K. Nehru was then the Indian High Commissioner in London and he and his Hungarian wife Fori invited us to stay at their luxurious residence. We moved in for a few days, but naturally couldn't stay there indefinitely. And we had no idea when we would need to come back, how long we would have to stay, what care I would need. We needed time to think this through, plan it, collect funds, and catch our breath. The Yugoslavian doctor calmed us down. 'Go home,' she said. 'Tumours don't grow so fast. Monitor Mallika's eyes, her peripheral vision, every week. The first change will be there when the tumour grows. Her peripheral vision will start to shrink. When you see the slightest change, plan on returning for the operation.'

We explained to Wynn that we needed time. He spelt doomsday. Unless we came back soon, he could do nothing. We returned home.

Amma was a great believer in the power of prayer. In those days, every Thursday, she used to visit a man called Babubhai, an unlettered and ordinary man in his real life. But every Thursday he was 'visited' by Shirdi Sai Baba, and would change completely, the way he sat, spoke, and suddenly started smoking beedis furiously. I have seen the transformation myself. One could never be sure when, on a Thursday, the possession would occur, but several times Amma and I were present when it happened. The room would fill with the fragrance of roses. The scent would become overpowering, and Babubhai would go stiff and glassy-eyed. He wasn't Babubhai any more. He was Baba. You could ask for his blessings or ask him questions to guide your decisions. Amma usually went alone. Upon our return from London with the frightening news, she headed straight to him. After a bit of thought he said to her, 'I do not see any ayudh (instruments) being used on her, so don't worry.' Amma hung onto these words over the months that followed. She certainly had great faith in him.

My weekly visits to the eye doctor began. My weight was still see-sawing but less radically. The thyroxine seemed to be having some effect in stabilizing at least the water retention that used to make me look and feel so bloated, and I started taking the diuretic Lasix every day. I also started being treated for a hormonal imbalance by Colonel Chopra, an ex-army man who was a famous homeopath. And Amma started poojas, and a search for alternatives.

Camellia Panjabi was an old friend, a Cambridge mate of my cousin Suhrid, and vice president of Taj Hotels. Her younger sister Namita was a friend of my brother Kartikeya and through him, of ours. At about this time, I got a message from Camellia that a healer from the Philippines was coming to conduct a three-day workshop at her home in Bombay. Did I want to attend? Sure I did. So off I went, not knowing what was in store but wanting to try all alternatives to surgery.

Swami Deva Leelananda (originally Dr Roland Carbonell) used to be a physicist with the MIT (Massachusetts Institute of Technology), working with NASA (National Aeronautics and Space Administration) in the US. And then he had his epiphany. His mother was a psychic surgeon in the Philippines, operating in the way I had seen in many documentaries, with her hands used as laser beams to separate out the atoms that make our skin and organs, and enter the body in mysterious but convincing ways. I have only faint recollections of the three days I spent there with Swamiji, but I was deeply moved and felt as though a load was off my shoulders. I invited him to Ahmedabad and he came.

I had my first brush with the supernatural or spiritual, I know not which. In his meditations, I felt one with the pulse of Prakriti, nature. I could go out to the garden and open up my arms and feel as though I was a conduit and the energy of the Universe was flowing through me into the earth and that I was a part of the eternal cycle. He did healings on me and I felt as though I was weightless. I was floating. I spoke at length of my grief at the loss of Papa, bottled inside me for so many years, and he listened. It was a strange period that helped me greatly. I continued seeing him in different parts of the world wherever our paths crossed, for several years after. Then, after nearly twenty years of being out of touch, in 2014, I looked him up on the Net, found a number for his daughter in NYC, called her, got his number and spoke to him. He has since passed away.

Meanwhile, back in Ahmedabad, someone tied a string around my wrist. Someone gave me mantras to recite. Someone else gave me powders to take. Then a friend of Amma's from England called to tell her of a coal miner in Manchester in whom an eighteenth-century surgeon took root every weekend, and how she knew of people he had cured. Did we want to come and try? He only worked on weekends, and it would take eight to ten sessions. Back we went to London, this time sleeping on the floor at Ashok's apartment, before moving in with Ruth Keshishian. Ruth, an Oxford friend of Ashok, was studying Sanskrit theatre. A gentle Armenian of great serenity, she had been shipped to England as a child in the 1940s when Armenia was still struggling against both the Soviets and the Turks. During our stay with her she introduced us to the joys of Lebanese food on Edgeware Road! Ruth later came to Ahmedabad and conducted research at Darpana with our resident scholar Govardhan Panchal, who was considered to be one of the greatest scholars on Sanskrit theatre. She has been running her parents' bookshop in Cyprus for the last couple of decades and we are frequently in touch.

Every Saturday morning we would take the train up to Manchester, to a working-class neighbourhood, and wait for the man. I remember one session clearly. His waiting room was an open terrace that had been converted into a waiting area. We walked into his dimly lit sitting room when our turn came. He barely spoke and his eyes were tightly shut. He indicated that I was to lie, face down, on his sofa. Under his breath he muttered instructions to an invisible nurse. Amma sat on a chair in a corner, watching. I heard him ask for a pair of scissors. Then a snipping noise, then he asked for pliers, then a needle and thread. Then he asked me to get up and said, 'I will see you next week.' We left. On the train Amma told me that he had mimed cutting open the skin along my spine, pulled things out and then stitched it up again. He had warned me that I might be sore the next morning. I wasn't. But all along my spine were suture marks in a bluish purple.

All through these two years I tried many things at the same time, many cures and faith healings. I wasn't really getting better but neither was I getting worse. Or perhaps I was just learning how to manage all the mishappenings within my body! In any case, my weight was still a huge problem, especially as I wanted to dance and do films. So in April, exactly two years since we left from Professor Wynn's clinic, we returned to London with the determination to get this sorted out, one way or the other. If it had to be through an operation, so be it.

The surgery was fixed for May 11, Amma's birthday. On the 8th, Professor Wynn sent a message to Amma that he wanted to see her the next morning, May 9, my birthday. We went to the hospital and Amma was called in alone. Wynn looked at her with his usual dour gaze and said, 'We won't do the surgery.' Amma's heart sank. Had we left it too late? Could nothing be done anymore? Wynn watched the emotions flit across her face, the fear and horror, and added, 'I mean, it is not needed. She will be fine.'

Amma nearly fainted with relief. But she could not understand what had happened. Wynn told her that the new multi-plenographs showed the tumour to be exactly the same as two years earlier and that no tumour, however slow-growing would do this. So he started to look for something similar by delving into articles and research papers and discovered nineteenth-century reports of a rare congenital malformation of the bone surrounding and protecting the pituitary gland, the pituitary fossa. He read that this malformed bone caused the gland to interpret it as a tumour, usually around the late teens. The message was conveyed to the brain and then to the body, which went into all the symptoms of an actual tumour before the brain realised that it was not a tumour and the body went slowly back to normal. He also mentioned that I was the first person in recent history who had been diagnosed as having this condition and that he wished to write a case study of an actual patient for medical journals! Go home, he said, everything will go back to normal.

I learned later that the medical term for the condition I had was 'the Empty Sella Syndrome'. The condition is now defined as a malformation of the bony structure that houses the pituitary gland. The bone cavity can be larger than normal or the gland smaller. It usually occurs in young or middle-aged women, and can cause loss of menstruation, pregnancy issues and other symptoms of a tumour. In most cases no treatment is necessary. In some, fluid needs to be drained through the nose. But little of this was known then.

The Empty Sella

But my issues remained. I still could not predict what I would look like the next day, whether I could film or not, whether or not I would be bloated or have headaches. Our friend Jamshed Bhabha stepped in once again and sent us to the research wing of the Memorial Sloan Kettering Hospital in New York City. Here the research team treated me as a rare subject, one on whom they wanted to try new drugs. The doctors put me on L-Dopa, a drug for Parkinson's disease that they had found to reverse the effects of a malfunctioning pituitary in mice! They said that it would help cut down the time that my body took to recognise that the 'tumour' was not a tumour. But, they warned me, I would probably never get pregnant, and if I did, it was unlikely that I would be able to produce any milk.

Later that year, the Darpana Dance Troupe went on a three-week performance tour to Sadler's Wells Theatre, London's prestigious dance venue. On the fifth night, Wynn and the entire department of endocrinology from St Mary's were in the balcony, and I could see Wynn gesticulating wildly to his colleagues to point me out as the Empty Sella Syndrome girl!

Over the next couple of years everything went back to normal. My hair stopped falling out, my skin returned to its normal texture, the headaches stopped, my periods became normal. And my weight stopped its mad gallivanting.

In 1984 I had the first of my two children, my son Revanta; and I breastfed both him and his sister who was born five years later.

And as Baba had promised, no ayudh touched me.

7
Dancing My Way Through Pregnancy

When I was being treated for my pituitary tumour, which turned out not to be a tumour but an 'empty sella' (see previous chapter), the doctors had warned me that I might never be able to conceive, a side effect of the drug L-Dopa which I was being given. Nonetheless, in January 1984 I found that I was pregnant. I also found out, on the same day, that I had contracted hepatitis.

A few weeks earlier I had performed at the Jail Auditorium in Coimbatore (I never found out why the jail had an auditorium). I came offstage between two items and asked for water. I was handed a glass. As I drank it, I clearly remember thinking, I hope it is safe. I am convinced that it was that glass of water that gave me the hepatitis.

Much later I was told that pregnancy and hepatitis together are a dangerous combination and that autism in the child is a high probability. I was not told then. What I was told to do was to take to my bed. I had no morning sickness. Instead I had such high bilirubin counts that my sheets turned yellow. I also had an unbearable itch all over my body. Amma and friends would clutch my hands tightly so that I did not lacerate myself scratching. We tried everything we could think of to stop or control the itch. Unguents, creams, poultices, desi, pardesi, home remedies, ash—you name it, it was tried. And failed. By complete chance a dear French friend, Chantale Forler, mother of a baby girl named Deborah Mallika in my honour, and wife of the ascetic French head of the new Alliance Française d'Ahmedabad, Achille Forler, asked me to try an anti-allergy cream from France that she always carried with her. That worked and gave me relief for a few hours. We needed to organise many tubes of it, in times before mobile phones, the internet, or even rapid couriers. Through the good offices of the French embassy in Delhi, and my friends' contacts there, a boxful arrived two weeks later, carried by a diplomat in his hand baggage.

Achille was of a deeply philosophical bent of mind and had run away from home in France to meditate in the Himalayas at the age of sixteen. After eleven years of meditation, learning Sanskrit and translating the Upanishads into French, he returned to society and India, in fact to Ahmedabad, to launch the Alliance Française there. On a break in Jodhpur he saw Chantale, a tourist on her first visit to India, across a fort, and their fates were sealed. They married and settled in Ahmedabad. Achille invited Amma to be the president of the AF. Having spent two years in Switzerland at a finishing school, Amma had a working knowledge of French and knew French literature and the art and culture scene well. Her career as a dancer too had been launched internationally in Paris, so there were many linkages and connections. She readily accepted and Achille and Chantale became family. We became their home, their path-bearers in finding their feet in Ahmedabad. This was going to be a long and very close friendship. Chantale's second pregnancy coincided with my first, which strengthened the bond.

The first four months of my pregnancy were spent in bed, turning yellow, with huge food restrictions, intermittent scratching, acute constipation and general irritation and boredom. I lost a lot of weight and that to me was the single plus point. I became bony, a size I had yearned for and never thought I would achieve.

By late April 1984, I had my doctor's permission to get out of bed and move around. I was planning on joining my then husband in New York in early May when my life took a dramatic turn. Out of the blue, one day, I received a telegram from the cultural attaché at the French embassy, someone I knew well, saying that the famous director, Peter Brook, and his team wanted to fly to Ahmedabad to meet and audition me for a part in their much-talked about international production, *The Mahabharata*. The script for the play had been written by Jean-Claude Carrière, a legend in cinema and theatre, who had written the script for such award-winning films as *Diary of a Chambermaid, Belle de Jour* and *The Tin Drum*. Carrière had accompanied Brook to India along with their co-producer, Marie-Hélène Estienne, the costume designer Chloé Obelensky and her assistant Pippa. Their journey across India and their meetings with many actors in search of the right cast to play the characters of Krishna and Draupadi had been much reported in the newspapers. As is usually the case, their search centred on the metros—the papers followed their journey from Delhi and Bombay to

Madras, Calcutta and Bangalore. So why me and Ahmedabad? I assumed it must be for some minor character.

The team came and after a short conversation, offered me the role of Draupadi. I was dumbfounded. Draupadi had always been my favourite character, feisty, unyielding, vocal. It was a role I could not refuse. But first I had to clear the auditions. I was flying to New York the next week in any case so my first audition was held there, with Brook's assistant, at the Lincoln Centre. Having passed that, I was flown to Paris, where, at Brook's theatre, Le Bouffes du Nord, I gave him an audition at 3 a.m. I had a flight back to NYC at nine o'clock. By the end of the audition the role was mine—if I would sign a two-year contract. I panicked, but after much introspection and persuasion from family and friends, accepted the role. The rehearsals were to start in September, the month the baby was due, and for obvious reasons I was given a grace period of five weeks. I needed to be in Ahmedabad during that period also because I had planned India's first international folk dance festival—Mahotsav '84—from October 4 for a week and could not abandon it and fly off to Paris, with 200 dancers from seven countries having been flown in, and a daily audience of 35,000 expected to attend—the cricket stadium had been chosen as the venue in anticipation. The festival was being held under the aegis of CIOFF (Conseil International des Organisations de Festivals), a UNESCO organisation. I had launched and become president of the Indian chapter of CIOFF in 1980, and Mahotsav '84 was the first festival being held in an Asian country.

Back in Ahmedabad after the US trip, and now clear of the hepatitis, I was allowed to get back to all my physical activities slowly and by the sixth month was dancing all out. My gynaecologist, Dr Behram Anklesaria, told me, 'Pregnancy is the most natural thing in the world. A woman's body is made to carry a child and do everything else normally. Complications are not the rule and behaving like an invalid is wrong. You are a strong and physically active woman so do what you would normally do.' I did.

Behram's parents were *the* gynaecologists of Ahmedabad in the 1950s and 60s. They had helped Amma with my birth, so in some senses I inherited Behram. A great lover of Western classical music, he was a gentle doctor and reputed to be a wonderful teacher.

My tummy didn't show till late into the eighth month so I continued performing. I had decided that I wanted to give birth at home, in my own bed. Labour started on the morning of September 1. Behram arrived and put on Tchaikovsky and said, 'Walk'. The labour lasted thirty-six hours and I marched till I dropped. As the pains grew, I screamed, 'Amma make the baby go back.' Revanta arrived at noon on September 2. I hadn't been able to eat once labour started, and once I had felt him lying on my chest, and he had been thumped and had screamed, all I wanted to do was to eat. Nuzzling the baby I wolfed down three idlis.

But the hepatitis took a toll on my son. I was breastfeeding him till his fourth month when he developed an intestinal infection that wiped out the intestinal lining. I was in Paris, in the midst of the worst winter in years, with frozen piping in my apartment, and the doctor wanted him hospitalised. I was terrified and convinced him that I would take all the care he needed at home, that as an Indian mother in Paris who spoke practically no French, I could not leave him in a hospital. Luckily he agreed and Revanta was nursed back to health. But I could not breastfeed him again, something that I regret till today.

As I had lost a lot of weight in the first five months, my total weight gain was only ten kilos. But my tummy was flabby and I needed to get back into shape. As I was breastfeeding, I couldn't go on one of my orange-and-Complan diets again, but I started on tummy strengthening exercises like crunches and sit-ups. It took me four months to come back to my normal size and shape, four months of a lot of walking, climbing steps and exercises. I also consulted a friend's 'miracle' nutritionist in Paris, who made me drink Van Houten chocolate powder in skimmed milk, eat a kind of ratatouille, and take weekly injections of artichoke extract into what I felt was cellulite. I doubt that any of that had the least effect but, ah, the Van Houten was delicious.

My second pregnancy in 1990 was a breeze compared to the first one. I was very careful to eat nutritious but not fattening food, so over the nine months I only put on eight kilos. I also continued my daily regimen of yoga and three hours of dance practice and swimming a couple of times a week. This time around too my tummy did not show and I was performing my one-woman solo show, *Shakti: The Power of Women,* till the end of the seventh month. I danced, jumped off tables, portrayed Rani of Jhansi in robust Kalaripayattu, with the full blessings of my doctor. Once I began to show, I stopped performing and started Kung Fu classes in Darpana. As the ninth month drew to a close I continued the martial art in the sweltering heat of an Ahmedabad May. The due date came and went. No baby. Kung Fu continued. On the 25th of May I finished the class at 8.30 p.m., and called Dr Anklesaria. The baby had to come, I told him, I couldn't take the load any more in 44 degrees Celsius! 'Drink a glass of castor oil and dance,' he said. I did, with Revanta, now five and a half. Two years earlier, in New York, I had studied Flamenco and Revanta decided that we would dance the Flamenco that night. So we did, till past midnight, furiously, and laughing in glee. Finally he fell asleep and I sat down to read. At 1.30 a.m. I felt the baby slide down and called Dr Anklesaria. He came, and by 3 a.m. Anahita was born.

The first delivery had lasted an excruciatingly long time, so this was almost as though nothing had happened. I asked Dr Anklesaria when I could dance. 'Tomorrow morning,' he said. So I did. And continued rehearsing, with Anahita strapped to my chest, till she learned to walk.

Breastfeeding is one of the most wondrous joys I have ever felt. It brought out a tenderness towards life and the world that I so wish one could bottle and sniff at, in stressful and anger-inducing times. And in my everlasting need to get back into shape, it made me lose weight rapidly.

My skin glowed, my face was chiselled, and I lost

the tummy flab very quickly. And that lasted long after I finished breastfeeding Anahita at fifteen months.

We have made pregnancy into an ailment. And rather than the pain and ultimate joy of a normal birth we seem to prefer picking a convenient time for a C-section. The women who do that without really requiring a C-section, are missing out on a unique experience. I could not have imagined that such acute pain was possible or that one forgot it the instant one held the baby in one's arms. But it is true, at least for most women. And it is a true miracle of the mind and body.

8

Training Tiny Muscles

The year 1984 turned out to be a momentous one for me. First pregnancy, first time as a producer of an international dance event, first international theatre job—and a dunking into the French language.

After I accepted the role of Draupadi in *The Mahabharata*, and before I left for Paris for the rehearsals and previews—the last few months of my pregnancy—I was busy doing multiple things. After the summer break at Darpana, at the end of June, I started performing again. I was in my sixth month of pregnancy and not showing at all. We were also preparing to host Mahotsav '84. And I was trying to familiarise myself with the playscript and French.

In the first year of college, at St Xavier's, Ahmedabad, learning a foreign language was compulsory. Amma spoke French fairly well. I loved listening to her speak to foreign visitors at our home, charmed by the musicality of the language, so I chose to learn French. A Spanish priest, Fr Echinez, taught us— French with a Spanish accent! Everyone except me had learnt French in school and was at a great advantage. I was lost. So I started going for private tuitions to a quirky, tiny English professor, a Parsi, who tutored for French, Professor Toos Vakil. At the end of the year, I knew enough to pass well but actually couldn't speak at all, except to say 'please' and 'thank you'! So, for *The Mahabharata*, I was in fact starting more or less from scratch.

The production was to be eleven hours long, and I had a long part—and five husbands and others to speak to in the play. So I needed to learn, and learn fast. Achille Forler generously took time off from his duties at the Alliance Française d'Ahmedabad and took on the task of reading and explaining the script to me and helping me learn my part before I left for Paris. And he tried and I tried and we managed to get me to memorise about half of what I was supposed to.

I arrived in Paris with five-week-old Revanta, five

weeks late for rehearsals as I had to be in Ahmedabad for Mahotsav '84. What with the pangs of leaving home for a long time, the exhaustion of the Mahotsav, a newborn baby that I was breastfeeding, and setting up home in Paris, I found it difficult to focus on the rehearsals. I had taken along help from India—Lizzy, my aunt Dr Lakshmi Sehgal's best-trained Malayali nurse, to look after Revanta. I had had the foresight to ask that my fees should cover the cost of her travel and stay, so finance was not an issue. Learning French quickly was.

To add to my discomfort, the group had bonded in the weeks before I arrived and I, as the only Indian, was looked upon with some trepidation and slight hostility. On the first day I got two shocks—the script that I had been learning with such earnestness was only provisional, and Achille's careful French was not what anyone in the group spoke. I couldn't understand most of the rapid-fire instructions and conversations, made more difficult as the actors spoke everything from Canadian French to that from Côte d'Ivoire. Luckily, Peter Brook's accent was very British, in spite of his many years of living and working in France, and he spoke with great deliberation.

About three weeks into this bewildering and daunting experience, Peter called me to his office.

'Your French has the possibility of becoming perfect. I want you to go to the Centre Tomatis for an hour every day. You don't need to do anything. Just go.'

I had no idea what this institution was, nor what to expect. And why would it make my French better? Armed with the address, I set off the next morning. I was expected and they took me into a room full of small booths with headphones, rather like record shops used to have in the days of vinyl records. There were lots of people in the booths, all wearing headphones, most with their eyes shut. I was placed in an empty one and asked to put on the headphones. 'Just relax,' I was told. 'Don't read.'

I put on the headphones. In each ear I began to hear different things. Music in one ear and text in the other. But sounding like a bad phone connection, unrecognisable, with some syllables heard and others not, scratchy, off again, on again. After a while I figured out that I was hearing a Mozart symphony in one ear and Antoine de Saint-Exupéry's *Little Prince* in the other. One hour went by. The earphones fell silent. I made my way out, baffled. Had this happened in the internet and Google period I would have looked up Tomatis immediately, but it was much earlier. Peter was pretty unapproachable but I asked everyone else

I met about it. No one had heard of it. I continued going, taking my knitting with me. Day after day I sat listening to gibberish—different some days, the same or similar on others. And with no idea how this was going to improve my French.

On the sixth day, at rehearsal, one of my French co-actors said to me, 'Your French is improving. How?' Soon everyone was noticing this and Peter just smiled. Once I had finished my one-month course, and everyone was telling me what beautiful accentless French I was speaking, Peter gave me a book about Tomatis.

Alfred Tomatis, a Frenchman, was born in France in 1920 and grew up in a musical family. Wanting to work with music and musicians he trained as an ear, nose and throat specialist. He developed a theory that many vocal problems were in fact hearing problems. That the voice does not produce what the ear cannot hear, became the bedrock of all his work. Soon he submitted the Tomatis Laws at the Academy of Sciences in France, proving the connection between hearing and phonation and hearing and communication. After a lot of research and many tests he developed what he called the electronic ear. He treated a famous opera singer, who had lost her voice completely and restored her magnificent voice through his treatment and

re-education. He presented the first electronic ear to the world at the Brussels World Fair.

Over the next two decades, Tomatis continued improving the electronic ear, and the range of applications also widened, from curing emotional and learning disorders to language difficulties. He realised that learning a language demanded the perceptual understanding of the musicality of the language. Soon the electronic ear was customised to suit every individual's need. He developed headphones with bone conductivity to reach the brain in a more efficient manner.

Research into bettering and perfecting the technique continued. By the time I started the course at the Centre, new parameters like delay, laterality and new filters had been added. Several books had been written on aspects of the method and on the research into hearing, translated into many languages. A training centre was started in Switzerland and the Tomatis Listening Test System had been developed to exactly gauge each individual's issues. Centres had also opened up in the US, England and other countries and professionals were being trained on the many and growing uses of the technique. Once digital sound was born, the analog sound that the method used switched to it, and the system improved greatly with the better quality of sound. The time for each session was shortened.

Dr Tomatis passed away in 2001, and his son and then his partner continued research for the expansion of the system and its applications. The first centre in India opened in Auroville around 2010, while I was a member of the Auroville Governing Council. The promoters, Mita Radhakrishnan and Tapas trained at the Tomatis Centre in Mexico and were delighted that I not only knew of the system but had greatly benefitted from it. They now treat a lot of patients with autism, depression, dyslexia and other learning disabilities. They also help the many foreigners in Auroville learn and perfect their Tamil.

So what did the gibberish do and why was it gibberish? Tomatis' theory claims that our ears only develop those micro muscles in the ear which are exercised from birth. In India, most of us speak at least three languages, and our ear muscles for these are exercised. Beyond the range of sounds in these three, our ears can't even hear the nuanced sounds of other languages. While learning a language, to get the accent correct, those particular micro muscles are awakened and trained. So more or less automatically, you begin to sound different, better, because unbeknownst to you, you are hearing the language differently, and reproducing what you hear. Voila, my excellent French. Next time you wish to learn a new language properly, and speak it like a local, head for your nearest Tomatis Centre.

9
A Coloured Life

Gujarat was embroiled in what appeared to be a genocide of the Muslims in the year 2002.

Following the violence unleashed by Lal Krishna Advani's Rath Yatra to raise funds for the building of the Ram temple after the demolition of the Babri Masjid in Ayodhya in 1992, work to collect funds and rope in volunteers, kar sevaks, for the building of the temple was in full swing by 2002. A train full of kar sevaks returning from Ayodhya was allegedly set ablaze by Muslim miscreants at Godhra on February 27, 2002, resulting in the death of fifty-eight kar sevaks. What followed was a well-planned carnage of the Muslims that altered Gujarat forever.

As I have mentioned in the chapter on smoking, I was amongst those who took the state government and the police and administration to the Supreme Court for what I believed was their role in the carnage. Over the next many years various people gave evidence, some who were in government service during the period and spoke once they had retired, some whilst still in government posts.

On April 14, 2011, nine years after the riots, Sanjiv Bhatt, a police officer who had been very close to the then chief minister, Narendra Modi, and who, in 2002, had been in the Investigation Bureau, chose to give evidence against the CM and the government, naming the CM for his involvement in the carnage.

The same year, he was taken to jail for a very old case. Many of us felt that his speaking out against the CM was the only reason that a case that been decided in his favour close to thirty years earlier, was suddenly reopened. Civil society organisations in Gujarat called for a rally to protest against his bail being turned down for no reason. I decided I must join them. Many colleagues and friends were present. The media was there in full force. I was given a handful of helium balloons to release into the sky. I was holding them aloft when someone came close to me with a lit candle. There was a loud noise, like a gunshot. The balloons had exploded in my hand, singeing my hair, burning my chest and right hand. By sheer luck, just before the explosion, a reporter to my left asked a question and I turned to him, saving my eyes and face.

A long and painful recovery period ensued. I had a national dance tour the week after the accident, so my daughter coated the thick bandage on my right arm, with the fingers all bound together, with skin-coloured make-up, painted on a gold bangle and decorated it with bright red alta. I did a strange version of arm movements sans hand gestures in all the performances across many cities. But the back of my palm remained nearly black many months after I had been proclaimed healed.

I have a light-coloured birthmark on the back of my left palm, much fairer than the rest of me. And now I had a blackened, mottled right hand. I was not pleased.

That year I had been working with European pianist Elizabeth Sombart for a collaborative performance by both of us, directed and filmed by Darpana's Artistic Director, Yadavan Chandran. I had met Elizabeth the previous year when I had been invited by her husband to the first Zermatt conference, 'Towards a Common Good', in Switzerland. Founded in 2010 by Swiss businessman and philanthropist, Christopher Wasserman, the Zermatt Summit is an annual forum of business leaders, thinkers and innovators that promotes the importance of business values and ethics in a globalised world.

On the first evening, before the formal welcome dinner, Elizabeth gave a piano recital. Both Yadavan and I were struck by her posture and breathing. It was as if she was playing as much with her breath as with her fingers. Intrigued, I spoke to her about this and asked if what we thought was true. Yes, we were told, she practised pranayama because she believed that the breath was a connection to one's soul, and that music had to come from there. We talked a lot over the next few days, and out of these conversations was born the idea of a performance on violence against women. We named it 'Women with Broken Wings'.

Several months post the conference we found ourselves working on the show in Lausanne in Switzerland, where Elizabeth lived. Noticing my burnt hand she enquired about it and said, 'Oh, you must meet my friend Bruno. He does light therapy and I am sure he will cure it.'

A few days later we were in Bruno Tournier's clinic. Yes, he assured us, light therapy can be used to reduce the discoloration post burns. He treated my hand with first blue and then yellow light for about four minutes. He gave me an ointment to apply on the affected area and asked me to come for a second session four days later. I went. Unfortunately there was no time for a third sitting, which he felt would be of help.

Over the next few weeks my burn mark started turning paler and soon my skin went back to its normal hue.

All of us have favourite colours. We have clothes that make us feel cheerful and positive. Even our languages describe moods as colours—I am in the pink of health; I feel blue today; she is evergreen; and even yellow journalism for reporting that is jaundiced and biased. So it should be no surprise that colour has an effect on us, and can change our moods. How far a leap of faith is it then to accept that colours affect the physical body too?

The science (some will say pseudo-science) of using different coloured light for healing is called chromotherapy. Chromotherapy uses the visible spectrum, colours, of electromagnetic radiation to heal. Light is energy and we see colour when energy meets matter. The wavelength, frequency and quantity of energy for each of the seven colours—violet, indigo, blue, green, yellow, orange and red, collectively known

by the acronym VIBGYOR—are fixed. Chromotherapy uses these in their absolute or combined forms to heal different diseases from blood pressure to aigue (a fever, like malaria, that is marked by paroxysms of chills, fever and sweating recurring at regular intervals. In French, a 'fievre aigue' is a sharp or acute fever).

Chromotherapy is distinct from other types of light therapy, such as neonatal jaundice treatment and blood irradiation therapy, which are scientifically accepted medical treatments for a number of conditions, as well as from photobiology, the scientific study of the effects of light on living organisms. Chromotherapy still sits amongst 'alternate' therapies!

References to the healing powers of colour come from ancient Egypt, China, India, Greece and also from Ayurveda. In ancient Egypt paint, sunlight and colour were used, with gems, stones, flowers and other material from nature providing the colours.

In ancient Greece, according to Samina Azeemi and S. Mohsin Raza,[*] the physical nature of colour was predominant and they used pigments, dyes and paint to cure. Later many of these cultures discovered

---

[*] *A Critical Analysis of Chromotherapy and Its Scientific Evolution* by Samina T. Yousuf Azeemi and S. Mohsin Raza, pub. 2005, https://www.ncbi.nim.nih.gov, HYPERLINK "http://www.hindawi.com"www.hindawi.com

the healing properties of water treated by sunlight filtering through coloured glass, and this became a popular form of treatment. At different periods of time different materials such as glass, silk, parchment and rice paper have been used to filter the light onto the body. In the last couple of centuries, different coloured rooms, made with glass or mirrors and with different forms of sunlight or artificial light filtering through, became popular.

Perhaps the most comprehensive work in the field was done by Dr Edwin Babbitt (1828–1904), scientist, mystic, physician, artist and essayist. In 1876, he published his book on colour, *The Principles of Light and Color*. He had two purposes for publishing his book. The first was to convince other doctors that he had discovered a valuable therapeutic system. The second was to present to the world a philosophy of 'light and color' that he believed described the basis of all life.

Babbitt presented 'a comprehensive theory of healing with color (sic)'. He identified the colour red as a stimulant, notably of blood and to a lesser extent the nerves; yellow and orange as nerve stimulants; blue and violet as soothing to all systems and as having anti-inflammatory properties. Accordingly, Babbitt prescribed red for paralysis, physical exhaustion and chronic rheumatism; yellow as a laxative, emetic and purgative and for bronchial difficulties; blue for inflammatory conditions, sciatica, meningitis, nervous instability, headache, irritability and sunstroke.[*]

In 1933, an Indian-born American scientist, Dinshah P. Ghadiali, greatly influenced by the work of Dr Babbitt, shed a lot of scientific light on the subject with his book *Spectro-Chrome Metry Encyclopaedia*[†]. He developed a range of twelve colours. He claimed to have discovered the 'how' of chromotherapy and why different coloured rays have various therapeutic effects on organisms. He believed that the application of colours to organs could rebalance them and bring about a healthy state. According to Ghadiali, colours represent chemical potencies in higher octaves of vibration, and for each organism and system of the body there is a particular colour that stimulates and another that inhibits the work of that organ or system. Ghadiali also thought that, by knowing the action of the different colours upon the different organs and systems of the body, one can apply the correct colour that will tend to balance the action of any organ or system that has become abnormal in its function

---

[*] Ibid.
[†] Pub. Dinshah Health Society, 1997.

or condition. His son Darius Dinshah continues to provide guidance on treatments through his Dinshah Health Society and his book, *Let There Be Light*.[*]

Ayurveda believes that if one is under stress, or there is an imbalance in the doshas, colours can help harmonise emotions and promote peace of mind. Ayurvedic medicine is based on the idea that the world is made up of five elements—aakash (space), jala (water), prithvi (earth), teja (fire) and vayu (air). A combination of each element results in three humours, or doshas, known as vata, kapha and pitta. These doshas are believed to be responsible for a person's physiological, mental and emotional health.

Every person is said to have a unique ratio of each dosha, usually with one standing out more than the others. According to healthline.com, essentially: 'Vata consists mostly of the two elements air and space (also known as ether) and is generally described as cold, light, dry, rough, flowing, and spacious. Those with the vata dosha are usually slim, energetic and creative. They are known for thinking outside the box but can become easily distracted. What is more, their mood is highly dependent on the weather, people around them, and foods they eat.

---

[*] Pub. Dinshah Health Society, 2005.

'Kapha (pronounced "kuffa") is based on earth and water. It can be described as steady, stable, heavy, slow, cold, and soft. People with this dosha are described as strong, thick-boned, and caring. They are known for keeping things together and being a support system for others. Kapha-dominant people rarely get upset, think before acting, and go through life in a slow, deliberate manner.'

The third dosha, pitta, is 'known for being associated with a tenacious personality; the pitta dosha is based on fire and water. It is commonly described as hot, light, sharp, oily, liquid, and mobile. People with pitta are said to usually have a muscular build, be very athletic, and serve as strong leaders. They are highly motivated, goal-oriented, and competitive. But their aggressive and tenacious nature can be off-putting to some people, which can lead to conflict.'

Ayurvedic practitioners even suggest what room lighting should be—soft and not fluorescent, as the latter evokes negativity and stress.

According to the website ayurvedichealth.com, colours can be used to treat specific conditions as each colour has attributes that trigger feelings and organs.

Black: Stimulates the ability to resist negative emotions. Excessive use increases fear and paranoia, and increases all doshas.

Blue: Encourages independent thinking and spirituality; shrinks tumours; can reduce fevers; acts like an antibiotic; neutralizes anger; cools emotions and regulates sleep. Too much can lead to a loss of compassion, sky blue can reduce the vata dosha and increase all other doshas.

Brown: Stabilizes. Excessive use coarsens the personality and reduces subtlety and refinement.

Gold: Increases self-awareness and spirituality; stabilizes the mind; strengthens the cardiovascular, immune and endocrine systems. Too much of it can reduce vata and kapha and increase pitta.

Green: Calms the mind and nerves, reduces fevers and headaches, balances the metabolism and stabilizes weight. Excessive use increases kapha.

Grey: Promotes objectivity and neutrality and cools the emotions. Too much can lead to depression and a loss of vitality.

Orange: Increases energy and intelligence, helps with thyroid issues and menstrual problems. Excess use of the colour can aggravate sexual problems and reduce vata and kapha.

Purple: Promotes confidence, reduces angina and eases joint stiffness. Excessive use can suppress and stagnate emotions.

Red: Boosts the cardiovascular system and increases energy. Too much increases neutrality and cools emotions, reduces kapha and increases vata and pitta.

Violet: Immunity boosting and antibiotic. The flip side is that it can suppress emotions.

White: Reduces fever and is an antibiotic, anti-viral, pain reliever; calms heat, emotions and stress; promotes compassion and vitality and increases spirituality. Too much can cause lethargy and hypersensitivity, increases inhibitions and kapha and reduces vata and pitta.

Yellow: Motivates and promotes clarity of the mind, improves communication and boosts energy. Excessive use can cause hyperactivity, lack of focus and depth; reduces vata and kapha and increases pitta.

Over the last twenty years interest in and practice of many alternate therapies has increased and solid research is being undertaken especially in Europe with France, Germany and Switzerland leading the research.

Padma Gulur, MD, professor of Anesthesiology and Population Health, Vice-chair, Duke University, believes that, 'Colour and light therapy have been used to treat a variety of conditions of both physical and mental health. Bright light therapy is used in mood and emotional disorders, such as depression, and green light has been shown to decrease the severity of migraines. Our research focuses on the use of green-coloured glasses to improve pain and decrease the use of pain medication, specifically opioids. We have also found that green light has a positive effect on anxiety.'* She is currently doing an NIH-funded (National Institute of Health) study on colour therapy.

In recent times there has been a proliferation of spa and cosmetic therapies using chromotherapy. Several years ago, from an airplane magazine, I picked out a device that transmitted orange and green light, guaranteeing a decrease in skin pigmentation. I used it for over six months and found a definite decrease in the pigmentation on my cheekbones. But the device broke down and replacement devices did nothing for the returned pigmentation.

The Covid-19 pandemic and the lockdowns brought a halt to clinic-based cosmetic therapies relied on by millions of people. Recognising a huge new market for 'home treatments', cosmetic companies have launched a series of products and devices using light and colour rays that people can use in their own homes. From face

---

* Quoted in the 2005 study *A Critical Analysis of Chromotherapy and Its Scientific Evolution* by Samina T. Yousuf Azeemi and Mohsin Raza, www.hindawi.com; *Evidence-Based Complementary and Alternative Medicine*, Volume 2, Article ID 254639.

masks that cover the entire face and radiate different coloured lights leaving you to choose which colour to use to solve your issues, to pen-like devices, the market is opening up. Many medical devices have also come into the market, transformed from hospital to personal use. What works needs to be seen.

While doctors around the world who scoff at any form of alternative medicine, evidence notwithstanding, may call chromotherapy 'quackism' and other names, in a world where more and more ancient wisdom is finding Western scientific proof, a time will come when this therapy will be as accepted and practised as yoga is today.

10

Mudslinging

Being reprimanded for eating mud is one of my childhood memories. I loved it. Whenever my friends and I played in the mud, especially in the dark clay of my paternal grandparents' home in Ahmedabad, or the red clay of Amma's maternal home in Chennai, I remember sucking on my fingers. And being told that it was a dirty habit and mud was for making things, not eating. It was several decades later that I discovered the therapeutic aspects of mud—including eating it.

We call the earth Mother Earth, Dharti Ma, Gaia. In naming her so, we acknowledge her capacity to eternally nourish us. But it is not merely a metaphorical use of the term 'mother'. History tells us that the nourishing capacity of the earth, call it mud or clay, has been used by humanity and animals for millennia, to make themselves whole again. Like other 'new age' systems of medicine, this too has been around probably since the beginning of human life as we know it.

As with chromotherapy, the earliest references to the use of mud for therapy are seen amongst the Egyptians, who used clay to mummify bodies and preserve them for hundreds of years. According to *Clay Cures* by Anjou Musafir and Pascal Chazot[*] ancient Greeks used to treat fractures with clay. The Persian polymath, Ibn Sina, known in the West as Avicenna (980–1039 CE), who is regarded as one of the most significant physicians, astronomers and thinkers of the Islamic Golden Age, and the father of early modern medicine, describes various kinds of clay used for medicinal purposes in his era.

Many African tribes have used clay on the body in decorative forms, but healing by clay is an ancient practice followed by them. Naturopaths in India have been treating patients with mud baths, hip baths and mud poultices for a range of ailments including skin diseases as well as organ-related or mental ones. Again,

---

[*] Pub. Mapin Publishing, 2006.

in many parts of Asia, Latin America and Africa, pellets of different clays are still sold and eaten by lactating and pregnant women and people suffering from mouth ulcers, toothache and other ailments.

Many different types of clay have been used over the centuries, with different clays gaining popularity at different times and for different cures. Today, across the world there are several forms of clay in therapeutic use.

Multani Mitti (Fuller's Earth): This contains silicate of alumina, magnesia and iron oxide. It is a variety of *Bole Armoniac* with astringent, refrigerant, absorbent and antiseptic qualities. It is yellowish and very gluey. Traditionally any clay used medically was called 'bole' and this one was found in Armenia and other places. References to it are found from ancient times. Theophrastus (371–287 BCE), the Greek philosopher who was Aristotle's student and regarded as his successor, Dioscorides (40–90 CE), the Greek physician, pharmacologist, botanist and author of *De Materia Medica*—a five-volume Greek encyclopaedia about herbal medicine and related medicinal substances—and Pliny the Elder (23/24–79 CE), the Roman author, naturalist and philosopher who wrote the encyclopaedia, *Naturalis Historia* (Natural History), have all made references to the use of this type of clay. Externally, Multani mitti or Fuller's Earth was used for dislocated joints, to treat bleeding and dysentery.

When I first started practising clay therapy twenty-five years ago, it was hard to find good-quality Multani mitti, and it came in large chunks that took a couple of hours to dissolve and become useable. With the new awareness of the worth of things organic, it is now available cleaned and powdered and easy to use, from organic stores.

Gopichandan: Thus named because it comes from a lake called Gopi near Dwarka in Gujarat, this is also a form of *Bole Armoniac*. For Krishna bhaktas or devotees, this is a sacred mud. It is available as small tablets and is most often seen on devout foreheads! It is high in magnesium iron and is traditionally mixed with water or rosewater and applied to ulcers and sores.

Geru: This is the red clay the Chinese call kaolinite or kaolin which in Hindi is called geru. According to Musafir and Chazot this is 'a native white aluminium silicate and iron oxide found in Sri Lanka and China, obtained by purifying native white fulspar or aluminium silicate by elutriation which removes the silica and under-composed fulspar. Thus it can be converted into a soft, whitish and earthy mass.'* Geru is often used in the preparation of Ayurvedic medicines. The same geru is also used to paint walls and clay pots. It is rarely used internally.

Green Clay: This is a green purified clay, very popular in France and easily available. The French use this for external and internal injuries and for application and ingesting. It is easily available in any French pharmacy.

White Clay: This is an expensive clay and is mostly used in cosmetics. Many of the readily available cosmetic clay masks to tighten pores and stop acne, use this.

Calcium Montmorillonite: According to Musafir and Chazot, this clay takes its name from the region of Montmorillon in France, and is considered a living clay. Unfortunately very few deposits are left of this around the world.* It is used mostly to set bones and for sprains and muscular issues.

In addition, of course, is perhaps the world's most famous clay, that from the Dead Sea in Israel. For centuries people have thronged this region and floated in the thick waters of this sea for cures. Its mud can

---

* Anjou Musafir and Pascal Chazot, *Clay Cures: Nature's Miracle for the New Age*, Mapin Publishing, 2006.

be found in packages large and small, primarily to be used as a layer on the skin, to be bathed off after it is dry.

Clay has the capacity of adsorption and absorption. Adsorption is the process of attraction, binding and accumulation of molecules or particles to a solid surface in a condensed layer. Absorption results when a substance diffuses or penetrates into a liquid or solid forming a transition zone or layer, often with a new composition, adjacent to the substrate. Clay minerals are ubiquitous in nature and their adsorptive and absorptive capabilities have been exploited in a variety of cosmetics and pharmaceutical formulations.

Scientific research into what actually makes clay work in so many different ways has been relatively scant. One of the great difficulties has been to create long-term teams of professionals from fields as far apart as geology, geophysics, cosmetology, alternative ancient medicines and allopathic doctors and researchers. One hopes that with the general 'going back to basics' wave across the world for all matters dealing with health, this research will soon find funders to facilitate it. Meanwhile, from personal experience I know that it works miraculously.

Different kinds of clay can vary in preparation time as it can dissolve in water differently. The Multani mitti organic powder that I use now takes just a few minutes to dissolve. This has to be done avoiding all metals as metals nullify the curative minerals in clay. I use a glass bowl and a wooden spoon to bring the clay to the consistency of play dough—thick enough to stay like a laddoo, but still moist. This clay can be placed on the skin where the problem is—on the forehead for a headache or on the liver or intestines for problems of that area. It can also be placed like the aforementioned laddoo on the arm and secured with a cotton bandage. It must be left there till it dries and then replaced. For an occasional headache or stomach ache one or two sessions should suffice, but for more serious chronic states, I have learned to keep moist mud on the arm more or less for twenty-four hours, for several days till a definite change for the better is seen. Often, in really bad cases, like for irritable bowel syndrome or very high blood pressure, I have treated people with a round-the-clock clay bandage for as long as two weeks, before going on to a regime of eight and then six or four hours a day till all symptoms disappear.

The great thing about all these therapies that I use on myself and others is that there are no side effects. Pranic healing cannot harm. Nor can mud. Well worth a try.

11

With a Little Help from My Friends

I started reading about alternate medical philosophies after I learned Transcendental Meditation or TM in 1974. Papa's death three years earlier had left me shattered inside and I had never really allowed myself to grieve. I thought Papa would have expected me to be strong for Amma, to protect her now that he was not around. But it was as though there was a gaping hole in me, an emptiness. A feeling of betrayal that he had died and left me, and always the question—why did he have to die?

In May 1974, I happened to be in Chicago where

I met Barbara Bennett, a young student of dance studying for her MA at UCLA, the University of California, Los Angeles. Her father was an important and wealthy real estate baron and Barbara was as close to being the Jewish Princess one reads of in novels, as can be. She wanted to know about my work and I started telling her about Darpana and Amma's work in using classical dance as a language to speak of issues that bothered her in today's world. Barbara was fascinated and asked if she could come to Ahmedabad and work with Amma. She asked her Dean for permission to come to India and make Amma's work the subject of her thesis. As fate would have it, her Dean was Allegra Fuller Snyder, daughter of the world-renowned architect and designer Buckminster Fuller. Both Allegra and her father were close friends of Amma's and had been of Papa's. Barbara was granted permission to go ahead with her thesis and arrived to stay with us in Ahmedabad a couple of months later.

As we grew closer she spoke of her work as a yoga and meditation trainer in the ashram of Maharishi Mahesh Yogi in Massachusetts. One day she said to me, 'Let me teach you TM. I think it will help.' I agreed. In the first session I found myself weeping uncontrollably, and then falling asleep and waking up twenty-four hours later, to a different feeling of reality. Something inside me had shifted. I felt I could breathe properly after nearly three years. I had three more learning sessions with Barbara after this.

I started meditating regularly, TM in the a.m. and the p.m. Twenty minutes of feeling myself go deeper and deeper into aloofness from the world, of feeling my body go into a floaty weightlessness. Of getting up after the session refreshed. I meditated regularly for the next twenty-five years, going into this deepened state, no matter what my surroundings and how much the noise. Then, for no reason that I can remember, I stopped for a few years but now I am back to it. Through times of intense fear, anxiety and stress, of great unhappiness or confusion, my meditation has calmed me, given me focus. Over the last year another friend has tried to initiate me into Sri Aurobindo's meditation, but I still find mine better to turn to.

Over the next many years, Barbara became committed to teaching yoga, developing yoga that wheelchair-bound people could practise and became more involved in research in the field. She also changed her name to Bija, seed.

Back in '74, Bija also started talking to me of Ayurveda and yoga, and of her mentor and senior, Dr Deepak Chopra. She aroused my curiosity and over the next ten years, I read up a great deal about non-allopathic ways of healing. My first successful brush with another system, however, had been much earlier, at the age of eleven or twelve, when I had a chronic sore throat. A cousin of my grandfather Ambalal Sarabhai, a prosperous cloth merchant, was also a noted homeopath and Amma, fed up of my having to resort to antibiotics every few weeks, took me to him. I remember being asked what I thought were strange questions, like, did I prefer cold or hot water for a bath and did I like hot food or cold food. I found the questions unrelated to sore throats, but he gave me sweet sugar pills to take, or at least, that is what I thought they were. After about six months of his treatment my sore throat was gone, and while I still sometimes get one, I have never had a chronic issue with my throat since then.

My next brush with homeopathy was a few years later. I developed terrible acne all over my face and hated it. I tried all the creams and unguents in the market. I tried drying the pimples with egg whites, with dahi (curd) and haldi (turmeric), with lemon juice. I used to conduct experiments on the two sides of my face by using Clearasil on one side and Lacto Calamine on the other, to see which dried the pimples faster. And I could not stop going to the mirror and bursting pus-filled pimples—oh, the sweet satisfaction! But none of this stopped the acne. Then Amma and I heard of a homeopath called Captain Madanlal, a retired army captain. And off we went to see him. Over a period of four months he treated me with auto-immune vaccines—vaccines made from the very pus of my pimples, to be taken as injections twice a week. He also gave me an ointment to put on the pimples. And it worked. Slowly my face started looking less angry. The pimples diminished in size and then nearly disappeared. Nearly. It was only when I became pregnant for the first time in 1984, that I became totally acne-free. And I have never had a pimple since.

In the mid-1990s I happened to meet the sugar baroness daughter of the gentleman at whose invitation I had given a dance recital at the Coimbatore Jail Auditorium in 1984. Raj Pathy and I became close friends. Like me she was interested in Indian systems of medicine. As Coimbatore has a very famous Ayurvedic hospital, we decided to try a proper three-week Panchakarma there one summer.

Panchakarma is a way of cleansing the body after lubricating it. It involves five ('panch') treatments and derives its name from this. It has preventive, curative and promotive benefits. These five karmas are:

Vamana: Therapeutic emesis or induced vomiting.

Virechana: Purgation to clear the lower gastric tract.

Anuvasana: Enema using medicated oil.

Nasya: Nasal instillation of medicated substances.

Asthapana Vasti: Therapeutic decoction enema.

I will come back to Panchakarma later in this chapter.

We went to visit the hospital where Raj knew several senior doctors but upon examining the rooms, felt hesitant to check in for three weeks. Raj, who had a sprawling house outside the city, decided to set up a therapy room at home where the doctors and therapy staff would come to treat her, Amma and me every day.

Ayurveda is considered to be the oldest system of health care, with literature going back 5,000 years and an oral tradition that is much older. This healing system has been practised in daily life in India for more than 5,000 years.

'Ayur' means 'life' and 'veda' means 'science'. Thus Ayurveda is the 'Science of Life'.

In Ayurveda, health is a state of spiritual and physical attainment. It is a medical, metaphysical healing life science—the mother of all healing arts. The practice of Ayurveda is designed to promote human happiness, health and creative growth. It is a system of knowledge that is said to have evolved from the sage Patanjali's practical, philosophical and religious illumination, which was rooted in an understanding of Creation. Ayurveda helps the healthy maintain health, and the diseased regain it.

Ever since those three weeks at Coimbatore, I have been hooked on my annual Ayurvedic retreat. After doing Panchakarma at Raj's home for many years, I met the remarkable holistic doctor Issac Mathai in 2001, through a friend in New York (Lynn Franklin, a literary agent, another Maharishi Mahesh Yogi follower, and a friend of Bija's). I was deeply impressed by his attitude and his credentials. His mother, Annamma Mathai, was one of Kerala's most famous homeopaths. Issac trained as a homeopath in Kerala and then at the Hahnemann College of Homeopathy in London. He then studied Chinese pulse diagnosis and acupuncture at the WHO Institute of Traditional Chinese Medicine in Nanjing, China, and did a course in mind–body medicine at the Harvard Medical School.

He returned to India, and started his practice in Bangalore for day patients. But his dream was bigger. He wanted to create a first-rate, world-class centre for holistic healing. When I met him, he had recently bought a large piece of land outside Bangalore, in

Whitefield, and was setting up Soukya, a holistic health centre. He believed that different forms of 'alternative' health systems needed to work in conjunction with each other to bring maximum health benefits to people. Having been variously cured over the years by a variety of health systems, I too believed this. So off I went with a friend to the still nascent Soukya.

On a sprawling and yet to be built campus, a fledgling team of doctors and therapists treated us for twelve days. Only the administrative block was complete and therapies went on in makeshift rooms. We were the first live-in clients at the new campus, although not in the city centre space from where the doctor had been operating.

By now I had been dancing and travelling full-time for a couple of decades, and felt that my body needed servicing once a year to keep it in top shape and perfect health. Niggling pains and the occasional sciatica apart, I really was aiming at 'future-proofing' my body for the hard dancing and touring routine that I knew would continue for years to come.

We started the day with wheatgerm juice and yoga, followed by breakfast and two to three hours of therapy. The afternoon consisted of lighter treatments, Swedish stone therapy or hydrotherapy or acupressure. Or a naturopathy pack for the liver (ah, the liver!).

With a Little Help from My Friends

The food was varied and Issac's wife, Suja, the resident nutritionist, interior and landscape designer, took great care to use all the organic ingredients from the garden to cook food from many states and continents. Breakfast was ragi idli or dosa for me, and when on a liquid diet to lose weight, liquid oats. Lunch and dinner were vegan. For me, they consisted of a variety of soups.

I felt cleansed, lost weight and came away rejuvenated. I have been going there ever since, mostly once annually for ten to fourteen days. It is my gift to myself and to the incredible body that allows me to continue dancing and soaring year after year, a thank you to my body.

The Covid lockdowns, however, put a stop to my Bangalore visits. In 2020 I missed a body servicing completely and started looking for alternatives closer home. I discovered a lovely nature cure centre close to Ahmedabad, Nimba. At the time of writing I have been there three times, for ten days once and five days twice subsequently and am now recommending it to all my friends.

Here are the treatments I take at Soukya for different periods, every year.

Abhyanga

Abhyanga is the application of oil or other lubricants all over the body. It must be done over the head, ears and feet. This is used as a preliminary treatment for Panchakarma and palliative (sodhana and samana) purposes.

During the massage, the direction and pressure of the movements in relation to the muscles, lymphatic drainage, vital parts, joints, abdomen, and especially in relation to the heart and circulation are of prime importance. A knowledge about the origin and insertion of the muscles and joint structure helps in determining the direction of the massage. Which oil is used depends on the patient and the season. Its many benefits include delaying the aging process; improvement of the quality and texture of the skin; improvement in the circulation and tone of the muscles; relieving tiredness and enhancing the quality of sleep. It also helps in peripheral neuropathy or the treatment of weakness, numbness and pain from nerve damage, usually in the hands and feet.

Narangakizhi

This is a treatment specifically for cervical spondylitis. Poultices primarily made out of lemon and other herbs are used for this treatment. These poultices are heated and massaged on the neck and shoulders using the appropriate oil as the base. This treatment reduces stiffness and pain and swelling around the neck; helps reduce pain in the shoulders and arms and numbness in the fingers and it stops arthritic changes in the cervical vertebra.

Shirodhara

Shira means head and dhara means the continuous maintained flow, or stream of liquid. The continuous pouring of a stream of liquid that could be made up of medicated oils, decoctions, milk, buttermilk, or herbal juices on the forehead at a specific height, period of time, and temperature is called shirodhara.

Shira is one of the most vital parts (marma region) of the body and is considered to be a route to all motor and sensory activities of the body. By regulating the functions of the head all the physiological functions are balanced and disorders set right.

The flow of liquid continuously on the centre of the forehead stimulates the function of the pituitary gland. The pituitary is the master gland, so it can influence all the other endocrine glands, thereby bringing about a total hormonal balance. This brings about a balance in the metabolic activities of the body. (My Empty Sella must benefit! See Chapter 6.)

Shirodhara also has an effect on the hypothalamus situated at the base of the brain. Because of this, it helps strengthen and tone the entire nervous system, the central as well as the autonomic nervous system, hence, all the vital organs of the body. The heart, lungs and brain get toned and the vital functions such as breathing, heart rate and blood pressure become normalised. This way the biological systems of the whole body return to normalcy.

Shirodhara combats stress and gets rid of its harmful effects. According to the philosophy of yoga, the sixth chakra—Ajna chakra, or the chakra of command, lies in the forehead. Dhara helps in strengthening this chakra which induces and strengthens the individual's commanding powers, ability to make the right decisions, strengthens the mind to face the ups and downs of life and makes the mind and body very strong. Dhara has many benefits: it relaxes the mind and eases depression, anxiety, hypertension and addictions; improves memory by stimulating the prefrontal lobe; facilitates tranquillity; is excellent for all neurological diseases including cerebro-vascular and neurological disorders; controls and slows dementia; helps in nerve disorders and much else.

Choornaswedam

This treatment involves fomentation with poultices made up of herbal powders. It can be with or without oil, depending on the nature of the ailment being treated, and the constitution or strength of the patient. This treatment reduces arthritic changes and stiffness; helps in losing weight; opens up the micro channels of the body; makes the body feel lighter and reduces fat deposits under the skin

Udvarthanam

This is a special type of massage with herbal powders and specific pressure in the pratiloma region (from the feet towards the heart). It helps to reduce and prevent excess fat in the body. Besides this, it strengthens body tissues and organs.

Elakizhi (Patra Pinda Sweda)

Patra means fresh medicinal leaves, and pinda sweda means poultice fomentation. This is a special type of massage done with poultices made of medicinal leaves. Here, medicinal leaves of a specific quantity are cooked in medicated oils. After being cooked for a certain amount of time, the leaves are made into poultices which are dipped in medicated oil and heated, then used for massage with fomentation. This is another treatment excellent for joint stiffness and to increase mobility and flexibility. It reduces sciatica pain and helps in the elimination of toxins.

Apart from these treatments, I also use some from naturopathy. This system believes diseases are caused by the accumulation of toxins. Prevention and elimination of toxins is the route to good health. Naturopathy uses the healing powers of nature: earth, water, air, fire and ether to heal. Treatments are designed based on these elements. There is no role of internal medication in naturopathy.

Liver Pack

This is the combination of castor oil pack and hot mud pack to the liver area. It detoxifies the liver and enhances its functioning; improves digestion and lymphatic circulation and increases blood circulation to the liver and abdomen.

I also undergo some Chinese therapies:

Reflexology

This is an Eastern healing technique used to relax the nerves and release trapped energy. There are energy zones that run throughout the body and reflex areas in the feet that correspond to all the major organs, glands and body parts.

Using thumb and finger pressure, the vital points in the feet and palms are pressed (also rotation of the patient's digits, and stretching of the skin on the soles and palms, and other movements). This is done on the bare skin of the feet and palms. Reflexology is believed to reduce stress and induce deep relaxation, improve circulation, cleanse the body of toxins, vitalise energy and strengthen the immune system.

Acupressure

This is a natural healing technique that uses applied pressure to relevant points of the body, thereby releasing any energy blockages. It is used both as a preventive and curative therapy.

Special emphasis is given to the back and neck. Acupressure relieves blockages, releases trapped nerves, restores balance, stimulates the circulatory and lymphatic systems and pushes certain brain chemicals to boost the immune system. It is also excellent to counter depression.

Panchakarma

As explained briefly earlier, Panchakarma means five types of treatment. The treatment happens in three stages:

1. Purvakarma: Preparatory procedures that help the body discard the toxins present in the stomach and tissues and help facilitate the toxins to move to the alimentary canal.
2. Pradhanakarma: The main treatment which is designed according to each person's individual's needs.
3. Paschatkarma: Post treatment care includes diet regimen and the other dos and don'ts.

This five-fold purification therapy aims at correcting the imbalance of the doshas—vata, pitta and kapha, in order to maintain their inherent equilibrium. During each season of the year, one or more of the doshas accumulate, which causes an imbalance and makes the body prone to illness. The five-fold treatment during Panchakarma eliminates disease-causing toxins but also replenishes the tissues with nourishment. This is why it is often called rejuvenation therapy. It combats neurological ailments such as paralysis, arthritis, rheumatism, dermatological problems and mental disorders.

Matra Vasti/Anuvasana Vasti

The word 'vasti' literally means 'that which stays inside the body for some time without causing any harm'. It is administered through the anus using medicated oil or ghee. Snehana dravya, or oil is the main ingredient in anuvasana vasti. The quantity and selection of the oil depends upon the constitution of the patient and severity of the disease being treated. The oil absorbs the toxins in the body and is thrown out as faecal matter after a while. It is excellent for digestive problems, joint and muscle stiffness and is said to help infertility.

For the last few years, while at Soukya, I have been going on a liquid fast for between seven to nine days and although it is tough to start with, it makes me feel great. Starting with the wheatgerm juice or another concoction prescribed by the doctor, I have liquid oats and honey for breakfast. Then halfway through the morning therapy comes a coconut water. Lunch and dinner are soups, usually two or three to choose from. They range from ash and snake gourd to amaranth, cabbage, spinach and mushroom. In between, whenever I am hungry or at least every three hours, I can have a vegetable juice, a thin buttermilk (allowed once a day), or another coconut water. And plenty of water. Now I try and do the same at home, a long one or periodic short ones, at least a couple of times a year.

In 2002 I started developing skin pigmentation on my cheekbones. I was told that this could be a side effect of long-term use of thyroxine, a drug I had been on since my Empty Sella days. As not using it was not an option for me, I had to find a solution. I tried the home remedies of aloe vera and lime, red sandalwood and haldi, but nothing seemed to work. A friend directed me to the famous Dr Jamuna Pai, skincare specialist of the beauty queens. I went to consult her. She started treating my skin externally and over the next few years the problem lessened.

I have always been curious about new treatments that are non-invasive, so over time I tried Botox (good for a forehead overworked because of Bharatanatyam abhinaya), fillers (made my face look fat), CoolSculpt (finally got rid of the love handles that had defied all exercise for decades) and Threads (painful but great to get rid of that slightly slackened jaw line). And then, a few years ago, I discovered face yoga.

Fumiko Takatsu, the founder of the face yoga method, had an accident that left her face totally distorted. In the year she spent having surgeries, she tried to research and delve into what could give her back her face. A practitioner of yoga, she started studying the musculature of the face. If yoga can cure the body, why could it not the face? This, she says, was the birth of face yoga. As soon as I found her and her method, a penny dropped. Why of course, this was obvious. I had seen the effects of yoga on my body and the same had to work for the face. I started on her basic set of exercises the very same day. And the next morning I could see the slightly tightened jaw. In one day? I could not believe it. There were exercises for every part of the face and neck, those that relaxed and those that tightened. After two years of daily face yoga I found that she had done further research and had developed more specific exercises for 'problem' areas like the nasolabial folds and drooping eyelids. I bought her digital book and follow the exercises meticulously, scrunching up my face every single day as I read the newspaper, making sure no one is terrified by what I am doing, not even my ever-present dogs. And I thank her with all my heart—and face.[*]

My wonderful gynaecologist, Behram Anklesaria,

---

[*] Fumiko Takatsu, *The Ultimate Guide to the Face Yoga Method*, CreateSpace Independent Publishing Platform, 2013.

the same one who told me to go play football during my pregnancy if I so wished, made me a potpourri of vitamins and minerals when I was beginning menopause, and with some changes, I still have a fistful of pills and capsules every morning. The only actual drug I take is thyroxine, and I have taken it for over forty years. The dose has varied from a high 4 mg to 1 mg for the last twenty years. Other than that here is what I take every day:

Fifteen or so years ago, I was introduced, by chemist and long-time Darpana Bharatanatyam dancer, Dr Minal Daftary, to a 'powder' made up of equal parts of dried ginger, amla, methi and turmeric. In Ayurveda and in naturopathy (and in all home remedies) these four are known to cure a range of ailments—and to prevent them, from high blood pressure to arthritis. They also clean the blood and provide antioxidants. I take a heaped teaspoonful with water every morning, making sure that the ingredients are from a certified organic store.

I have had chronic constipation since I was about eleven or twelve. Amma started me off on Milk of Magnesia tablets. I then went on, for several years, to Isabgol. Then when I was sixteen, a friend introduced me to Baidyanath's Ashta Virechan Choorna. His father had had it for years and was really happy with it. I started with two teaspoons and a glass of water just before bedtime every night. It worked like a charm. And has for several decades. I have never changed the dose, never had to increase it. Over my many sessions of Ayurveda various doctors have tried to sort the chronic issue by giving me ghee, vasti and whatnot, and none of it works. I also defy the common beliefs on why constipation happens—when one does not drink enough water, does not eat enough roughage or does not exercise enough. In all three cases I err on the side of excess. Over the years I am fine with taking my choorna every night. It is not an addiction and I don't fret over it unless I have early flights or shoots with no guarantees of clean loos. Then, I skip taking it. Other than that, all is well.

Sometime in the late '90s another family friend, the Jesuit P. Rappai, retired vice principal of my college, St Xavier's, and a true believer in an alternate lifestyle in all things, introduced Amma and me to Pranic healing. More about that elsewhere in the book.

In 2009 I decided to fight the Assembly elections as an independent candidate from the constituency where I have lived all my life. It happened to have Lal Krishna Advani as the sitting MP. For a month my life, and that of everyone who joined the campaign voluntarily or unwillingly, was crazy. I started off on the campaign trail at 6 a.m., holding public meetings in many of the 220 villages that formed part of my constituency, besides large swathes of Ahmedabad and Gandhinagar. A few days into my campaigning, one of our night guards, who taught drawing in a school by day, came to me and asked if I knew of magnetic bracelets. Only vaguely, I said. He pulled out a pamphlet from his pocket, professionally printed and in English, that explained how, with all our mobile devices, mobile towers, computers and myriad gadgets, we are surrounded by electromagnetic waves that are detrimental to our functioning. It stated that thus drowned, we were operating at around 30 per cent of our capacity. As a solution it offered a titanium-lined bracelet that would protect us from these waves. 'Can I have ten minutes of your time to demonstrate this to you?' he asked. Over the next few days I made the time. He sat me down on a chair. He then gave a bracelet each to four of my colleagues to wear. He asked them to try and lift me from four sides using only their index finger. And they did. I was way up in the air on four fingers! After I finished campaigning, I went to a lecture about this, organised at a venue in the city. The speaker explained the science, showed some slides, did the lifting exercise with several volunteers. I decided to give it a try. I was convinced it could do no harm, even if it did not increase my energy and strength levels. I bought a bracelet.

It was May and the heat was intolerable. I was waiting for the election results and rejoined a Kalaripayattu class in Darpana. On the third day the teacher took me aside and said, 'Your kicks are higher than ever and you are so much more flexible. What are you doing that is different?' There was only one thing that was different. I was wearing the bracelet, albeit as an anklet.

In 2022 I am still wearing it. And I truly believe that it has made a huge difference to my levels of energy and my stamina. Some time ago I was performing in Dehradun, and was surprised at how tired I became after just an hour of dancing. It was the same for the next performance. I started getting concerned. Was I eating wrong? Why had my energy levels dropped? Was I missing out on vitamins? Then I noticed that the bracelet was not on my ankle. I searched everywhere but could not find it. I have now replaced it and am back in my usual form. It is now easily available online as a health bracelet. And it is not bad-looking.

Over the last year I have also restarted oil pulling, something I did regularly years ago. It consists of swishing around raw oil in the mouth for ten minutes, first thing in the morning. I use coconut oil. This too is an old Ayurvedic kriya that cleans out the toxins in the mouth and protects the teeth. Practitioners believe that a lot of toxins from undigested food lodge in our mouths overnight and this kriya stops them before they re-enter the stomach.

A very important aspect of my wellness are my dogs. I first bought Freddy, my miniature Dachshund, when my daughter was a year old, thinking it would keep her and her older brother occupied when I was on tour. In fact Freddy became my third child. Since then we have always had between four and nine dogs. And I adore them. When I am fighting with the world, when everyone disapproves of me or what I am doing, their love and devotion is unwavering. They always greet me as if I had been away for years. They nuzzle. They keep close if they feel I am sick or unhappy or in floods of tears; they know. They come and lick me to make me feel better. I can hold them and feel renewed. Yes, they are an important help, and my truest friends.

12

Healing Others

We are all used to visual representations of spiritual people or gods and goddesses with halos around their heads. But is this just a flight of fancy of the creator of the image or is there any basis for this?

We have all also had instances where, without reason, we feel repelled by or attracted to someone. Is this instinct or is there something more to this? And are the two examples I have just given related or unrelated?

The idea of an ethereal body or an aura, or a sukshma sharira, exists in many ancient philosophies including ours. In his book *The Human Aura*, Walter J. Kilner writes, as quoted in *Miracles Through Pranic*

Healing by Choa Kok Sui, the founder of Pranic healing and Arhatic yoga, 'Sacred images from early Egypt, India, Greece and Rome, used this convention before it became popular in Christian art, and before the aura was considered an attribute of ordinary everyday mortals...For centuries it has been believed that clairvoyant people could actually see an aura surrounding ordinary individuals, and this aura differed from person to person in colour and character, expressing the health, emotional and spiritual attributes of the subject. The visionary Swedenborg (Emanuel Swedenborg, the Swedish theologian, philosopher and mystic) wrote in his *Spiritual Diary*: "There is a spiritual sphere surrounding everyone as well as a natural and corporeal one".'

Southeast Asia was under the Indian sphere of cultural influences from about 290 BCE till the 1500s. Unlike many Hindu kingdoms that banned travel across the seas, the powerful southern empires of the Pallavas and Cholas sent armies and monks, teachers, traders and artisans to the East, travelling all the way from Burma to China and Japan. In each of these countries they left influences of their land, and in each country these combined with the local culture to become unique cultures. This was true of dance and music, architecture, cuisine, martial arts—and healing. Reiki, Pranic healing and psychic surgery, each developed in a different country, are variations on the theme of healing through the astral bodies' connections with the physical body. Each of them works on the astral body to heal the physical body or the mind.

In the early '90s I was sent a leaflet on Pranic healing with the announcement of a course in Ahmedabad. It was being organised by a Sister Elizabeth of the Jesuit Society. Having had my earlier brush with psychic healing when I was trying to cure my pituitary tumour (as I had been told it was), I was keen to learn. Amma and I decided to enrol.

Pranic healing as we know it today was codified by Grand Master Choa Kok Sui, who was born in Cebu in the Philippines. It believes that everything has an energy body, not seen by most people but present just outside our physical body. If the energy body is disturbed or uneven, the corresponding body part will get sick. The two bodies are very closely connected as is the mind and the two bodies. Clairvoyants can actually see astral bodies, the colour and thickness indicating the health of each part.

In 1939, Russian electrical engineer Semyon Kirlian discovered, by accident, how to photograph the aura. He and his wife happened to be standing next to a patient at the Krasnodar Hospital who was being treated with a high-frequency electric generator. Kirlian saw that when the electrodes were close to the patient, there was visible a glow around the patient. Repeating the process at home, he noticed the same glow. Experimenting further, he put different objects, for example a book, on a metal sheet that acted as the conductor and connected another conductor to the book. A film negative or photographic film was inserted between the conductor and the book. When an electric current was passed through the conductor it produced an image around the book. Kirlian tried photographing both animate and inanimate objects, trees, plants, cutlery and animals and human beings. Fearing sceptics, he didn't make his work known to the public till twenty years and hundreds of experiments later. Today many scientists have worked on updated versions of the camera and holistic healers regularly use aura photographs to improve patients' health.

Auras are energy channels that circulate around the body. Pranic healing consists of learning how to channel the energies of nature, through the healer and into the patient. There is energy all around us, in the earth, in the air, in the oceans and rivers, in trees and plants and in the sun. The healer learns to take in this energy and focus it on the patient. According

to Pranic healing, ill health can occur in one of two ways, when there is a congestion of energy in one place or when there is a depletion. The healer learns to scan the patient's body with her hands to assess the health of the aura, its evenness around the entire body, and then channels energy into problem areas.

Pranic healing works with the chakras or the meridians through which traditional medical systems believe the body is monitored. Just as the physical body has organs, the energy body is divided by chakras that rule different parts of the body. There are eleven major chakras, and many minor and mini chakras. Major chakras are whirling energy centres. They are believed to be like power stations that supply energy and health to the physical organs.

Chakras absorb, digest and distribute prana, energy, to the different parts of the body. They are responsible for the healthy functioning of the entire physical body. Major chakras control the endocrine system which in turn controls the organs and the way they function.

The basic or **root chakra** is located at the base of the spine, in the coccyx. It controls, energises and strengthens the entire physical body: the muscular and skeletal systems, the spine, the production and the quality of blood, the adrenal glands, the tissues of the body and of the internal organs. It also affects the sexual organs. It affects body temperature, general vitality and the growth of infants and children. Its malfunctioning can cause arthritis, spinal and blood ailments, cancer, leukaemia, allergies, growth problems, low vitality, and slow healing of wounds and broken bones. People with a highly activated basic chakra are usually quite robust. The basic chakra is like the root of a tree. If the root is weak, the tree is weak.

The **sex chakra** is located on the pubic area. It controls and energises the sexual organs and the bladder. Its malfunctioning manifests as sex-related problems. The ajna chakra, throat chakra and basic chakra have a strong influence on the sex chakra and can weaken or strengthen it.

The **Meng Mein Chakra** is located at the back of the navel. It serves as a 'pumping station' in the spine and is responsible for the upward flow of subtle pranic energies coming from the basic chakra. It controls and energises the kidneys and adrenal glands and controls blood pressure. A depleted Meng Mein can cause kidney and back problems, blood pressure and low vitality.

The **navel chakra** is located on the navel. It controls and energises the small and large intestines and appendix. It affects the general vitality of a person. Its depletion or congestion manifests as constipation, appendicitis, difficulty in giving birth, low vitality and other diseases related to the intestines. Energy is also called ki or chi. The navel chakra produces what is called biosynthetic chi. Different from other chi, this energy helps to draw in, assimilate and distribute other energies. An unbalanced navel chakra can disturb a lot of other body functions by starving them of chi.

The **front** and **back spleen chakras** are located on the left part of the abdomen between the front solar plexus chakra and the navel chakra, in the middle of the left bottom rib, with the back one directly behind it. These chakras control and energise the spleen and purify the blood. They also destroy worn-out blood cells. They are the major entry points of air prana. Air prana is digested by the spleen chakra and then distributed to the other major chakras and the entire body, thereby energising them.

The **front** and **back solar plexus chakras** are located at the solar plexus area, the hollow area between the ribs, with the back chakra directly behind it. This chakra controls and energises the diaphragm, pancreas, liver, stomach and, to a certain degree, the large and small intestines, appendix, lungs, heart and other parts of the body. This chakra also affects the quality of the blood because it controls and energises the liver which detoxifies the blood. Through the liver it controls the cholesterol level of the body and affects the condition of the heart. The solar plexus chakra is the energy clearing house of the aural body. Subtle energies from the lower chakras and from the higher chakras pass through it. The whole body can be energised through these. The solar plexus chakra also controls the heating and cooling system of the body. Malfunctioning can cause diabetes, ulcers, hepatitis, heart ailments and other illnesses related to the organs mentioned. The solar plexus chakra and the navel chakra control and energise the gastrointestinal system.

The **front** and **back heart chakras**: The front heart chakra is located at the centre of the chest and energises and controls the heart, the thymus gland and the circulatory system. Its malfunctioning manifests as heart and circulatory ailments. It is affected by the solar plexus chakra which is sensitive to emotion, tension and stress, and has a strong influence on the physical heart. The front heart chakra is closely connected to the front solar plexus chakra by several big energy channels, and is also energised by the front solar plexus chakra to a certain degree. Patients with heart problems usually have malfunctioning solar plexus chakras. The back heart chakra is located directly behind this. It primarily controls and energises the lungs and, to a lesser degree, the heart and the thymus gland. Malfunctioning of the back heart chakra manifests as lung problems such as asthma and tuberculosis. The whole body could be energised through the back heart chakra.

The **throat chakra** is located at the centre of the throat. It controls and energises the throat, the thyroid gland, parathyroid glands and the lymphatic system. It also influences the sex chakra. Malfunctioning of this chakra manifests as throat-related ailments such as goitre, sore throat, loss of voice, asthma and sterility.

The **Ajna chakra** is located exactly between the eyebrows. It controls and energises the pituitary and the endocrine glands. It is what we call the third eye. It is considered the master chakra because it directs and controls the other major chakras and their corresponding endocrine glands and vital organs. It affects the eyes and the nose. Its malfunctioning leads to diseases related to the endocrine glands like diabetes. Energising it can lead to an overall upsurge in energy.

The **forehead chakra** is located at the centre of the forehead. It controls and energises the pineal gland and the nervous system. Malfunctioning can result in loss of memory, paralysis and epilepsy.

The **crown chakra** is located at the crown of the head. It controls and energises the pineal gland, the brain and the entire body. It is one of the major entry points of prana. Its being depleted or congested can lead to diseases of the head or psychological upsets.

The crown and forehead chakras facilitate the harmonising and normalising of the other chakras, just as the pineal gland facilitates the harmonising and normalising of the other endocrine glands. The pineal gland affects the aging process.

The first practical process we were taught was how to open up our hand chakras. These are located in the centre of each palm and are the most accessible chakras. And these are the chakras we use for healing. By the end of the first day, having learned how to open these chakras we started trying with our hands to feel the aura of different people in the workshop. We were trained to clean and re-energise, and then turned loose in the unsuspecting world. It all comes with constant practice, we were told.

My children and dogs were my first experiments. The children constantly hurt themselves, or got a fever or a cold. I would do a healing, following procedures from Master Choa's books and the children would feel better. But I always wondered if it was psychological—till Revanta, my son, had a high fever. I sat for hours healing him, taking his temperature every half hour or so. And I saw it go down from 104 degrees to normal. That is when I started believing in my own ability to heal.

IN FREE FALL

Over the years I have worked with hundreds of people. Many have reposed such faith in me that they have made me do distance healings—something I first learned in 1994 when on tour in Hong Kong. I had left the children at home and got a long-distance call from Anahita, then aged four, bawling down the line. No, she would not go to a doctor, and no, I had to heal her. She had had a bad fall and besides bruises and cuts, had twisted her ankle. I had learned how to do this from the book, but could I? Apparently I could. A few hours later a very relieved Amma called me to say she was fine and not in pain.

I feel blessed to have learned this. And it can never be taken away from me.

13

Unmessing My Head

There have been times in my life when I have been very stressed or anxious or depressed and each time I have dealt with this differently. After Papa's death, transcendental meditation helped. After my engagement broke up and I went into a depression that lasted several months, I discovered dance and that healed me.

In early 2015 I was severely stressed and deeply unhappy. I had always been very close to my children and had been through hard times bringing them up alone after my husband and I separated. I did not want to put a strain on their relationship with their father, wanting always to be fair and honest, wanting them to develop as ethical, compassionate human beings. This was often a difficult line to walk. How much freedom is too much? How much experimentation with relationships is too much and when must I intervene? My dilemma increased when I myself got into a new relationship. I worried if they felt displaced—or worse, if they disapproved.

In 2002 my son Revanta left to do his Bachelor's degree in dance and film at the University of the Arts in Philadelphia and was away for four years. When he came back he wanted to learn choreography and creative arts, so he left again to do his Master's in performance and creative research at the University of Roehampton in London. He stayed on in London after his degree to work for a while. At some stage during this period, during one of his visits home, he said to me that he felt his father was very lonely and needed looking after so he wanted to move to his house for a few days. He had also mentioned a few times in earlier years that our apartment, situated within the Darpana premises, on the first floor of the building, was like living in a fish bowl, always being watched for who came in and out and when. The long and short of it was that he moved out, permanently. It was never discussed with me. I was never told. It happened. I have subsequently discussed it with him, told him of my feeling of hurt and rejection, and my perception that that was not the way to do things. The hurt is now healed—still without my knowing why he did it that way. But in the larger view, these are things I let go of, because we are still very close, work together and meet all the time.

In Revanta's absence, my daughter Anahita, younger by five years, and I bonded even closer. She came out as gay when she was fourteen and that was fine by me and the rest of my family, Amma included. Then she started being with older women, design students who were twenty-one and twenty-two years old, and I didn't quite approve. I worried that in their company, she may start doing drugs. She didn't like my disapproval, but we were close enough to be able to talk about it. In 2009 she too went away to college in the US, and would return twice a year. In her second year there she developed a serious back problem, and missed a year, spending it at home, trying various therapies including spending time with Dr Mathai at Soukya in Bangalore. Through all of this, we remained very close.

Then things started going wrong. I date this to 2013, but she to much earlier. My relationship with my partner was a problem for her. She also felt I favoured Revanta, when in fact my family constantly chided me for the exact opposite. She seemed to dislike the way I spoke to her about her needing to lose weight if she wanted to dance professionally with us. She thought I treated her friends rudely or brusquely. With every absence, the bond was breaking. We both said and did things to hurt the other. We stayed under the same roof but our individual bedrooms became the place to retreat to, far away from the other. She started having friends over whom I didn't know, getting more and more involved with the gay community. With her then partner, the daughter of an academician whom I respect greatly, she started a safe space for queers called QueerAbad, where every week people from the gay community would meet and discuss the problems and issues facing them. But Anahita and I stopped talking to each other. I could feel only hostility and disapproval when she was in the same room. Perhaps she felt the same. I felt I couldn't breathe in my only safe space, my own home.

Finally things came to such an awful stage that I had to ask her to leave—I felt strangulated by her presence in my home, and I couldn't continue living that way. My ex-husband, who was very close to her, tried to intervene and we had, or tried to have, one last dialogue. She denounced me, or what she felt I had become, as a mother. And moved in with her partner.

I was broken. I couldn't breathe. I felt suffocated. I couldn't sleep. I was anxious. This went on for a few months and nothing seemed to help. Finally I decided that no one except me could solve this, that I had to get hold of myself.

Everyone around me was involved because they loved us both and the broken relationship caused them pain. My dearest friend and partner couldn't really talk to me because he was part of my daughter's problem with me, and he too was emotionally involved with the situation. Amma was torn and I did not want to burden her with a break between two of her most beloved people. In any case, Amma had begun withdrawing from taking family matters into her own hands, beginning to give us the mantle in what she knew would be her last innings. Amma was 97. I knew she would be gone soon and that I would lose my closest soulmate. This was not a sorrow I wanted her to carry with her wherever her journey took her next. She passed away in January 2016, leaving me bereft.

Even some of my closest women friends could only console me that this too would pass, that she would come around, for they too knew her from when she was born. I needed desperately to talk to someone who was a trusted outsider involved in healing minds.

My son had, some years ago, dated a young girl he

grew up with, and whose mother I had known over the years although never as a close friend. I knew she had been involved in healing movements and was a seeker. One day she dropped by to see me, and my dam broke. She listened to me calmly, making me feel calmer, and then spoke to me of NVC—Nonviolent Communications, founded and developed by Marshall Rosenberg, and inspired by the strategies of Mahatma Gandhi. She sent me links and videos of how it worked. She spoke of how we can become aware of certain buttons or words that derail conversations, how we can learn to choose not to use them. Something in what she was saying seemed like a glimmer of hope so I started a serious study of it.

Also called Compassionate Communication, this non-violent way of living was developed in the US by Marshall Rosenberg in the '60s. It assumes that we are all basically compassionate people who resort to other violent strategies when we do not see success in being good and kind. When we find no good strategies to meet our needs, we turn to anger and violence.

According to his websites (cnvc.org and nonviolentcommunication.com.en.wikipedia.org) and his biography[*], Rosenberg was working at peace-making

---

[*] *Beyond Anger and Blame: How to Achieve Constructive Conflict*, *The Christian Century* by Allan Rohlfs.

during the Civil Rights Movement and needed a theory to explain violent behaviour. Non-violent communications or NVC as it is used today developed out of his extensive research between the mid-'60s and 1992, when the theory was classified as a system. Since then it has evolved and changed, laying greater emphasis on the process rather than the steps, and also on the intentions of the speaker.

The ultimate aim of NVC is to develop societal and personal relationships based on a restorative 'partnership' paradigm and mutual respect, rather than a retributive, fear-based 'domination' paradigm.[*]

To illustrate these differences in ways of communicating, Rosenberg started using two animals; the carnivorous jackal represented violence, aggression and dominance; the herbivorous giraffe represented NVC strategy. The giraffe was chosen as its long neck is supposed to represent the clear-sighted speaker, aware of what others are saying, large-hearted and compassionate.

NVC holds that most conflicts between individuals or groups arise from miscommunication about their human needs, due to coercive or manipulative language

---

[*] Marion Little, 'Total Honesty/Total Heart: Fostering Empathy Development and Conflict Resolution Skills', MA thesis, University of Victoria, 2008.

that aims to induce fear, guilt, shame and so on. These violent modes of communication divert attention away from problem solving thus perpetuating conflict.

There are four components in practising NVC:

Observation: These are facts, what we see and observe, rather than an evaluation of meaning and significance.

Feelings: Emotions and sensations free of thought and story.

Needs: These are universal needs of human beings.

Requests: A request is different from a demand, in that in a request one can negotiate even beyond a 'no'. In a demand a 'no' brings an end to the conversation or negotiation.

Then there are three modes for the application of NVC:

Self-empathy: This involves compassionately connecting with ourselves and truly facing what the needs are that are being or not being met.

Receiving empathically: Learning how to see the beauty in another person, their divine energy, their goodness.

Expressing honestly: Learning to name a need rather than a feeling, and making a request for its fulfilment.

I started regularly reading about NVC and watching the case studies acted out by the Bay Area NVC centre. I started seeing a pattern in what I said and what others said that led to anger and conflict. I learned to ask myself what I wanted to achieve at the end of a negotiation—to feel I had the last word? To make the other person feel diminished? To fill a need of mine? To come to a conflict resolution?

Over the last five or six years, I have tried these techniques—some to good results and others not so successfully. My rift with my daughter has not healed. But all the introspection has led to my being able to separate myself from an issue or hurt, and to be able to distance myself from the trauma. And I keep going back to the writing and the videos of the case studies. Had things not been disrupted by Covid, I would by now have also attended my first long workshop on NVC. It is a complex but wonderful technique that requires study and practice. Perhaps, like me, you might find it worth exploring in depth.

14

Occupying My Body, Making It My Friend

The Last Twenty Years

I write this chapter on the first day of the second week of the Covid-19 lockdown on April 1, 2020. I have not practised dancing for twelve days. I have restarted regular one-hour sessions of yoga only four days ago. I am not on a diet but am not overeating. I don't have the urge to do so. When I feel like a piece of dark chocolate, I have one. My body is treating me with respect and I am treating my body as my friend.

Have I been able to change my metabolism? Has

my body found itself and its equilibrium? When did this change happen—and is it a permanent one or just a temporary reprieve?

After the first thirty years of being consumed with the desire to be thin, my body started finding its own balance. I was dancing many hours. I was doing yoga. I had become a conscious eater, and while I wasn't consciously conscious of eating all the time, my mouth and appetite and my mind created an ecosystem where excesses were tempered with sensible eating, and where, even on a holiday binge of cheese and bread, my subconscious knew that I would go back to eating correctly, almost by instinct. And of course, once a year my holistic treatment at Soukya, to recalibrate everything.

Since I turned forty-five, I have also taken to having complete check-ups of body functions, eyes and teeth included, twice a year in January and June. These are sent to my three consulting doctors, Issac Mathai of Soukya, Dr Jayachandran, my resident Ayurvedic doctor, and Ashaben Patel, my local holistic doctor, a woman of instinctual healing powers. Each gives an opinion and they usually concur. Course corrections are sometimes needed as when D3 levels are low, and I take a course of the vitamin.

I measure my weight and fat levels twice a week.

I like to be at around 60–61 kgs with around 18 per cent fat. If it is tending upwards, I go on a five-day Soukya liquid fast. Besides cleansing the system and knocking off the excess, it also makes me feel virtuous, being able to stay off the delicious food all around me!

For my skin and face I tend to drum up home remedies and cures. Aloe vera, cream skimmed from milk boiled for the house mixed with lime and besan, avocado, honey and rosewater, tomatoes and potatoes, all find their way onto my face. Coconut and sesame oils, cold-pressed, are also always present on my bathroom counter. Organic vegetable- or fruit-based shampoos and soaps complete my routine.

The body is a quick learner, and if we leave ourselves open to listening to what it needs, we learn to steer a proper course. It takes time and training to be able to do that, but each of us has the capacity to do it, and know when external help is needed and must be sought. And it is necessary to be alert to changes and refer these to a doctor. Postponing consulting a doctor about a new growth, or roughened skin, or a series of inexplicable bruises is plain stupid behaviour. Letting the fear of something serious being discovered take over sensible behaviour is a recipe for disaster.

It takes time and patience to learn to listen to and hear one's body. I started many years ago by analysing

cravings and binges. If I suddenly crave for jalebis, what triggered it? A memory from the past? A wafting fragrance? Something I was reading or a conversation that brought back memories of a happy time while eating jalebis? This takes time and honesty. I would then try and examine if I was actually hungry. Then, whether the hunger could be assuaged by something else that was sweet but was healthy. If the answer was no, that I had to eat jalebis, I would first eat an apple and then buy only one jalebi, and eat at a rate where I consciously tasted, felt the texture and smelled the fragrance of the coveted jalebi. In this way I stopped myself gulping down a plateful of jalebis because I was craving, not really savouring them.

The process is hard but certainly possible. I urge you to try it and cultivate the sense of partnering your body and feeding it what it really craves—sugar or salt or spices. It is worth it.

Epilogue

The Comeuppance

I began writing this book a few days into the first lockdown in 2020. Over the next nine months, I worked on it and revised it. And then came my comeuppance in late September of 2020.

At 2 a.m. on the morning of September 24, 2020, I woke up from my sleep and could not move. My body seemed to have shrunk and frozen. I was in acute pain. I was alone with my dogs in the apartment on the Darpana campus, with two guards at the gate, one phone call away. But I was unable to stretch my hand to reach the phone.

Over the next four hours, I somehow managed to sit up, get on to my bottom, and 'bum walk' my

Epilogue

way to the door to let the dogs out. My body was screaming with pain. Chikungunya, my bedraggled brain told me. Having had friends and colleagues describe this mosquito-borne illness, I knew this was it. This could not possibly be Covid, the virus that had kept us all locked down.

Over the next two hours I managed to get help and a doctor, who took one look at me and confirmed the problem. He warned that high fever would come and a lot of pain, cheerily prescribed a paracetamol and assured me that there was no actual medication for CG!

In a few hours my temperature had shot up to 104 degrees. I was in agony. My children rallied round, continuously putting cold water compresses on my forehead. I could think of nothing and feel only pain, such pain as I had never experienced in my entire life. After four days of this the temperature came down. On the fifth day I felt normal again and went to my morning yoga class. By afternoon I was stiff and shrunk, and again in agony.

Friends suggested alternate remedies. Ayurvedic, homeopathic, home remedies. Various leaves, boiled and drunk. Some powders. More powders. Pain balm to ease the agony. I could not raise my hands enough to brush my teeth or comb my hair. My shoulders and back were in a vice. My neck could move slightly to the left or right. Then it got jammed.

I have never experienced anything like the pain and stiffness I did for the next two months. I had no appetite, and lost five kilos. My face showed the acute pain I was in. I shuffled. Climbing up or down stairs was impossible, as was opening a screwtop bottle, or even picking up a glassful of water. With all the good health and fitness I was used to, I was at the mercy of a mosquito. I was reduced to nothing. I could see my muscles losing strength, getting weak.

Did forty-plus years of carefully nurtured good health and clean living amount to nothing?

I realised many things. For the first time I could understand the sheer grit and willpower of people who live with constant pain, of those who, after accidents or birth defects, work for years to get back control over their bodies, and go on to do extraordinary things like climb mountains. And I realised the arrogance of thinking that we are in control of our bodies if we do things right. Yes, we can avoid many lifestyle diseases that are born out of our own treatment of our body, and that is a lot, for a majority of what ails fellow beings seems to be brought upon them by their own behaviour. But there are other things we cannot control. I do think that all my years of looking after

FAT, HOMEOPATHY MITHERAPY, HYPNOSIS
HYPNOSIS MICRO GREENS D3, HOMEOPATHY
THERAPY GREENS D3, HYPNOSI FAT, PROTINE
PROTEIN, MICRO GREENS,

my body as my temple gives me a fighting chance to recover from an illness, perhaps even to recover more fully and faster. But it is still fragile and prone to the unexpected.

Three months later, I was still struggling. I could not hold up the basic arm position of Bharatanatyam, nor sit in the basic stance of the aramandi. Under guidance from Iyengar yoga specialists, I had restarted yoga two weeks earlier, and could do a tiny bit better every week. Swimming as part of my physiotherapy, was helping and continued doing so. But I was still in pain, and my shoulders, arms and neck were still stiff. The mobility of my limbs remained greatly reduced as did my stamina. And having been in so much pain for so long, I remained afraid of more pain.

It took me more than fourteen months to make a partial recovery from chikungunya. With a lot of physiotherapy, various medicated oils, yoga and dancing, and occasional painkillers, I recovered 95 per cent of my shoulder movements. My shoulder still ached many hours of the day but the pain was just a fraction of what it had been. The reduction in pain and the widening of movement was slow and steady. But it took me another month or two to make a complete recovery.

Did this experience negate the way I have lived my

Epilogue

life, always with the aim of being well and healthy? No, not at all. I think we must try and do everything we can to help nature in keeping our bodies and minds in a state of health. And we must be prepared that it can all go for a toss because of a single virus, or gene, or mosquito. For the rest, life is a daily gamble anyway, so let's keep the dice as loaded in our favour as we can.

Acknowledgements

I would like to thank the accident or destiny that brought me to my parents, Vikram and Mrinalini Sarabhai, and the amazing DNA they carried and represented and passed on.

And my editor Renuka Chatterjee. I have edited so many others that being edited was quite an experience!

And friends and foes, the thousands who abuse me daily on social media and those whom I meet across the world, who squeeze my hand and whisper, 'You made me a different person, thank you'.

Appendix

My Daily Yoga Asanas

I am sharing here the asanas that we do every week at Darpana. There are some that we do every day: Four very slow and eight fast Surya Namaskars; pranayama; any two of the following asanas: Bhujangasana, Pavanamukhtasana, Mandukasana, Sarvangasana, Halasana and Shavasana. For the rest, they are performed any two days of the week, depending on what our instructor decides as the order. While online learning has become common, I still feel that learning from a trained teacher is very important, as is developing a series for your own physical and emotional needs.

When I do not have the time to do more than ten minutes, I prefer the Surya Namaskar routine as within it, it has so many of the asanas that make the spine and arms flexible. Here they are, with small explanations of their use, taken from B.K.S. Iyengar's *Light on Yoga*. I have kept to his spellings.

Vrksasana

Vrksa means a tree. Tones the leg muscles and gives one a sense of balance and poise.

Utthita Trikonasana

Utthita means extended, stretched. Trikona (tri=three; kona=angle) is a triangle. Tones the leg muscles, removes stiffness in the legs and hips, corrects any minor deformity in the legs and allows them to develop evenly. It relieves backaches and neck sprains, strengthens the ankles and develops the chest.

Parivrtta Trikonasana

Parivrtta means revolved, turned round or back. Trikona is a triangle. This is the revolving triangle posture. It is a counter pose to Utthita Trikonasana. The previous asana turned around. Improves the blood in the lower part of the spinal region, relieves pains in the back, invigorates the abdominal organs and strengthens the hip muscles.

Utthita Parsvakonasana

Parsva means side or flank. This is the extended lateral angle pose. Tones the ankles, knees and thighs. It corrects defects in the calves and thighs, develops the chest, reduces fat around the waist and hips and relieves sciatic and arthritic pains. It also increases peristaltic activity and aids elimination.

Parivrtta Parsvakonasana

The revolving lateral angle posture. Aids digestion and removes waste from the intestines.

Virabhadrasana I

The chest is fully expanded and this helps deep breathing. Relieves stiffness in the shoulders and back, tones up the ankles and knees and cures stiffness of the neck. It also reduces fat round the hips.

Virabhadrasana II

Strengthens and shapes the leg muscles. Relieves cramps in the calf and thigh muscles, brings elasticity to the leg and back muscles and tones the abdominal organs.

Virabhadrasana III

Contracts and tones the abdominal organs and makes the leg muscles more sturdy. Gives vigour and agility.

Ardha Chandrasana

Ardha means half. Chandra is the moon. Helps damaged or infected legs, tones the lower region of the spine and the nerves connected with the leg muscles and it strengthens the knees. Along with the other standing postures, this asana cures gastric troubles.

Surya Namaskara: Salutation to the Sun

A series of different yogic exercises done as a series that becomes the go-to asana if doing only one. It stretches and compresses most parts of the body.

Janu Sirsasana

Janu means the knee. Sirsa is the head. Tones the liver and the spleen, aiding digestion. Tones and activates the kidneys.

Paschimottanasana

Paschima means the west. Tones the abdominal organs and keeps them free from sluggishness. It also tones the kidneys, rejuvenates the whole spine and improves the digestion.

Paripurna Navasana

Paripurna means entire or complete. The posture here resembles that of a boat with oars, hence the name.

Ardha Navasana

Ardha means half. Nava is a ship, boat or vessel. This posture resembles the shape of a boat, hence the name. Works on the liver, gall bladder and spleen.

Purvottanasana

Purva means the east. Strengthens the wrists and ankles, improves the movement of the shoulder joints and expands the chest fully. It gives relief from the fatigue caused by doing other strenuous forward-bending asanas.

Ardha Matsyendrasana

Ardha means half. Matsyendra is mentioned as one of the founders of Hatha Vidya. Here the spine is laterally twisted. Benefits the lower abdomen and stops the enlargement of the prostate and bladder. The next step is the Purnasana.

Parighasana

Parigha means a beam or bar used for shutting a gate. The pelvic region is stretched, one side of the abdomen is extended while the other side is laterally flexed. This keeps the abdominal muscles and organs in excellent condition and prevents the skin around the abdomen from sagging. Helps stiff backs.

Dhanurasana

Dhanu means a bow. The hands are used like a bow-string to pull the head, trunk and legs up to resemble a bow. The spine is stretched back. Brings back elasticity to the spine and tones the abdominal organs. Combined with Salabhasana, it helps people with slipped discs.

Chaturanga Dandasana

Chatur means four. Anga means a limb or a part thereof. Danda means a staff. The pose strengthens the arms and the wrists, develops mobility and power. It also contracts and tones the abdominal organs.

Bhujangasana

Bhujanga means a serpent. The spinal region is toned and the chest fully expanded. Helps those with slightly displaced discs.

Parsvottanasana

Parsva means side or flank. Uttana means an intense stretch. Relieves stiffness in the legs and hip muscles and makes the hip joints and spine elastic. Abdominal organs are contracted and toned. The wrists move to dissipate stiffness. Corrects round and drooping shoulders.

Sirsasana

Considered the king of all asanas. Makes healthy, pure blood flow through the brain cells, rejuvenating them for enhanced thinking power and clearer thoughts. Tonic for people whose brains tire quickly. Helps with constipation.

Sarvangasana

It is one of the greatest boons conferred on humanity by our ancient sages. This asana is a mother of all asanas. Persons suffering from breathlessness, palpitation, asthma, bronchitis and throat ailments get relief. This asana is recommended for urinary disorders and uterine displacement, menstrual trouble, piles and hernia.

Halasana

Hala means a plough, the shape of which this posture resembles, hence the name. The abdominal organs are rejuvenated due to contraction. The spine receives an extra supply of blood due to the forward bend and this helps to relieve backache. Cramps in the hands are cured by interlocking and stretching the palms and fingers. People suffering from stiff shoulders and elbows, lumbago and arthritis of the back find relief in this asana.

Setubhandasana

Setu means a bridge and Setu Bhandha means the formation or construction of a bridge. This asana gives the spine a backward movement and removes strain on the neck.

Jathara Parivartanasana

Jathara means the stomach, the belly. Parivartana means turning or rolling about, turning round. This asana is good for reducing excess fat. It tones and eradicates sluggishness of the liver, spleen and pancreas. It also cures gastritis and strengthens the intestines.

Ardha Baddha Padmottanasana

Ardha means half. Baddha means bound, restrained, caught and withheld. Padma is a lotus. Uttana is an intense stretch. Stiffness of the knees is cured by this asana. As the abdominal organs are contracted, digestive powers increase and the peristaltic activity helps to eliminate toxins that create waste matter. The pose helps one to move the shoulders further back. This expands the chest and helps in breathing freely and deeply.

Garudasana

Garuda means an eagle. It is also the name of the king of birds. Garuda is represented as the vehicle of Vishnu and as having a white face, an aquiline beak, red wings and a golden body. This asana develops the ankles and removes stiffness in the shoulders. It is recommended for preventing cramps in the calf muscles. For removing cramps in the legs and for relieving pain the poses recommended are Garudasana, Virasana and Bhekasana, also called Mandukasana.

Salabhasana

Salabha means a locust. The pose resembles that of a locust resting on the ground, hence the name. The pose aids digestion and relieves gastric troubles and flatulence. Since the spine is stretched back it becomes elastic and the pose relieves pain in the sacral and lumbar regions. People who suffer from slipped discs have benefitted by regular practice of this asana without recourse to enforced rest or surgical treatment. The bladder and the prostate gland also benefit from the exercise and remain healthy.

Parsva Dhanurasana

Parsva means sideways. In this variation of Dhanurasana, one performs the posture lying on one's side. The sideways roll in this posture massages the abdominal organs by pressing them against the floor.

Urdhva Mukha Svanasana

Urdhva Mukha means having the mouth upwards. Svana means a dog. The pose resembles a dog stretching itself with the head up in the air, hence the name. The pose rejuvenates the spine and is specially recommended for people suffering from a stiff back. The movement is good for persons with lumbago, sciatica and those suffering from slipped or prolapsed discs of the spine. The pose strengthens the spine and cures backaches. Due to chest expansion, the lungs gain elasticity. The blood circulates properly in the pelvic region and keeps it healthy.

Adho Mukha Svanasana

Adho Mukha means having the face downwards. Svana means a dog. When one is exhausted, a longer stay in this pose removes fatigue and brings back the lost energy. The pose is especially good for runners who get tired after a hard race. Sprinters will develop speed and lightness in the legs. The pose relieves pain and stiffness in the heels and helps to soften calcaneal spurs. It strengthens the ankles and makes the legs shapely. The practice of this asana helps to eradicate stiffness in the region of the shoulder blades, and arthritis of the shoulder joints is relieved. Persons suffering from high blood pressure can do this pose.

Gomukhasana

Go means a cow. Mukha means face. It also means a kind of a musical instrument, narrow at one end and broad at the other like the face of a cow. The pose cures cramps in the legs and makes the leg muscles elastic. The chest is well expanded and the back becomes erect. The shoulder joints move freely and the latissimus dorsi are fully extended.

Supta Virasana

Supta means lying down. In this asana one reclines back on the floor and stretches the arms behind the neck. This asana stretches the abdominal organs and the pelvic region. People whose legs ache will get relief from holding this pose for 10 to 15 minutes and it is recommended to athletes and all who have to walk or stand about for long hours.

Baddha Konasana

Baddha means caught, restrained. Kona means an angle. This pose is specially recommended for those suffering from urinary disorders. The pelvis, the abdomen and the back get a plentiful supply of blood and are stimulated. It keeps the kidneys, the prostate and the urinary bladder healthy. It relieves sciatic pain and prevents hernia. The pose is a blessing to women. Pregnant women who sit daily in this pose for a few minutes will have much less pain during delivery and will be free from varicose veins.

Matsyasana

Matsya means a fish. The chest is well expanded. Breathing becomes fuller. The thyroids benefit from the exercise due to the stretching of the neck. The pelvic joints become elastic.

Yoga Mudrasana

This asana is especially useful in awakening Kundalini. Crossing the hands behind the back expands the chest and increases the range of shoulder movements. It intensifies the peristaltic activity and pushes down the accumulated waste matter in the colon and thereby relieves constipation and increases digestive power.

Ardha Baddha Padma Paschimottanasana

Ardha means half, baddha means caught, restrained, and padma a lotus. Paschimottanasana is the posture where the back of the whole body is intensely stretched. Due to the half lotus pose, the knees become flexible enough to execute the full lotus pose. The pose is recommended for persons with rounded and drooping shoulders.

Trianga Mukhaikapada Paschimottanasana

Trianga means three limbs or parts thereof. In this posture the three parts are the feet, knees and buttocks. This asana is recommended for persons suffering from dropped arches and flat feet. It cures sprains in the ankles and the knee, and any swelling in the leg is reduced.

Krounchasana

Krouncha means a heron. It gives a full extension to the leg and exercises the muscles of the legs. The abdominal organs are also rejuvenated.

Marichyasana I

This asana is dedicated to the sage Marichi, son of the Creator, Brahma. The fingers gain in strength by the practice of this asana. This asana creates a better circulation of blood round the abdominal organs and keeps them healthy.

Marichyasana II

As this pose is an intensified form of Marichyasana I, its effects are greater. The heel at the navel puts extra pressure on the abdomen so that the abdominal organs are toned better and grow stronger and digestive power increases.

Upavistha Konasana

Upavistha means seated. Kona means an angle. The asana stretches the hamstrings and helps the blood to circulate properly in the pelvic region and keeps it healthy. It prevents the development of hernia, of which it can cure mild cases, and relieves sciatic pains. Since the asana controls and regularizes the menstrual flow and also stimulates the ovaries, it is a boon to women.

Parivrtta Paschimottanasana

Parivrtta means turned around, revolved. Paschima literally means the west and refers to the back of the entire body from the head to the heels. Uttana means an intense stretch. This invigorating posture tones the abdominal organs and keeps them free from sluggishness. It also tones the kidneys and rejuvenates the entire spine, while the digestion is improved. The lateral twist stimulates blood circulation in the spine and relieves backaches. Due to the stretch of the pelvic region, more oxygenated blood is brought there and the gonad glands absorb the required nutrition from the blood. This increases vitality, helps to cure impotency and promotes sex control.

Ubhaya Padangusthasana

Ubhaya means both and Padangustha means big toe. To start with one rolls over backwards to the floor, and it takes some time and practice to learn to balance on the buttocks alone.

Akarna Dhanurasana

Karna means the ear. Dhanu means a bow. The practice of this posture makes the leg muscles very flexible. The abdominal muscles are contracted and this helps to move the bowels. Minor deformities in the hip joints are adjusted. The pose is full of grace.

Supta Konasana

Supta means lying down and kona an angle. This pose tones the legs and helps to contract the abdominal organs.

Parsva Halasana

In this pose, the legs rest sideways on one side of and in line with the head. This is the lateral plough pose. In this asana, the spine moves laterally and becomes more elastic. People suffering from acute or chronic constipation which is the mother of several diseases derive great benefit from this asana.

Eka Pada Sarvangasana

Eka means one, single. Pada means the foot. This asana tones the kidneys and the leg muscles.

Urdhva Prasarita Padasana

Urdhva means upright, above, high. Prasarita means extended, stretched out. Pada means foot. This asana is a wonderful exercise for reducing fat around the abdomen. It strengthens the lumbar region of the back, tones the abdominal organs, and relieves those suffering from gastric trouble and flatulence.

Supta Padangusthasana

Supta means lying down. Pada is the foot. Angustha means the big toe. This asana is done in three movements. The legs will develop properly by the practice of this asana. Persons suffering from sciatica and paralysis of the legs will derive great benefit from it. The blood is made to circulate in the legs and hips where the nerves are rejuvenated. The pose removes stiffness in the hip joints and prevents hernia.

Uttana Padasana

Uttana means stretched out or lying on the back with the face up. Pada means a leg. The asana gives full expansion to the chest wall and keeps the dorsal portion of the spine supple and healthy. It tones the neck and back and regulates the activity of the thyroid by ensuring the supply of healthy blood. The abdominal muscles are also stretched and strengthened.

Bharadvajasana II

The knees and shoulders become flexible by the practice of this pose. It is not very effective for people with elastic spinal movements, but the arthritic will find the pose to be a blessing.

Malasana II

Mala means a garland. By doing this posture the abdominal organs are exercised and gain strength. Women suffering from severe pain in the back during the menstrual period will obtain relief in this pose and the back will feel soothed. In this pose, the arms hang from the neck like a garland, hence the name.

Pasasana

Pasa means a noose or cord. The pose gives strength and elasticity to the ankles. Persons whose work entails standing for hours will rest their feet in this position. It tones the spine and makes one agile. The shoulders move freely and grow stronger. The pose reduces fat around the abdomen, massages the abdominal organs and at the same time expands the chest fully.

Vasisthasana

Vasistha was a celebrated sage or seer, the family priest of the Solar race of kings and the author of several Vedic hymns, particularly of the seventh Mandala of the Rig Veda. This pose strengthens the wrists, exercises the legs and tones the lumbar and coccyx regions of the spine.

Hanumanasana

Hanuman was the name of a powerful monkey chief of extraordinary strength and powers in the epic, *The Ramayana*. This beautiful pose helps to cure sciatica and other defects of the legs. It tones the leg muscles, keeps the legs in condition and if practised regularly is recommended for runners and sprinters. It relaxes and strengthens the abductor muscles of the thighs.

Eka Pada Rajakapotasana

Eka means one, pada the leg or foot and kapota a dove or pigeon. Rajakapota means the king of pigeons. This pose rejuvenates the lumbar and dorsal regions of the spine. The neck and shoulder muscles are fully exercised and the various positions of the legs strengthen the thighs and ankles. The thyroid, parathyroids, adrenals and gonads receive a rich supply of blood and function properly, which increases vitality. In these poses more blood circulates round the pubic region, which is kept healthy. These asanas are recommended for disorders of the urinary system and for controlling sexual desire.

Natarajasana

Nataraja is the name of Shiva as Lord of the Dance. This difficult balancing asana develops poise and a graceful carriage. It tones and strengthens the leg muscles. The shoulder blades get full movement and the chest expands fully. All the vertebral joints benefit from the exercise in this pose.

Savasana

Sava or Mrta means a corpse. In this asana the object is to imitate a corpse. Once life has departed, the body remains still and no movements are possible.

By remaining motionless for some time and keeping the mind still while you are fully conscious, you learn to relax. This conscious relaxation invigorates and refreshes both body and mind. But it is much harder to keep the mind than the body still. Therefore, this apparently easy posture is one of the most difficult to master. This removes the fatigue caused by the other asanas and induces calmness of mind.

Mandukasana

Manduk means a frog. The action in this asana resembles that of a frog, hence the name. The abdominal organs benefit from the exercise as they are pressed against the floor. The knees become firmer and the pose relieves pain in the knee joints due to rheumatism and gout. It also gives relief when there is any internal derangement of the knee joints. The pressure of the hands on the feet creates a proper arch so cures flat feet. It helps sprained ankles and strengthens them. The pose also relieves pain in the heels.

PRANAYAMA

Nadi Sodhana Pranayama

Nadi is a tubular organ of the body like an artery or a vein for the passage of prana or energy. A nadi has three layers like an insulated electric wire. The innermost layer is called sira, the middle layer damani and the entire organ as well as the outer layer is called nadi. The blood receives a larger supply of oxygen in Nadi Sodhana than in normal breathing, so that one feels refreshed and the nerves are calmed and purified. The mind becomes still and lucid.

Bhastrika Pranayama

Bhastrika means a bellows used in a furnace. Here the air is forcibly drawn in and out as in a blacksmith's bellows. Hence the name.

Ujjayi Pranayama

The prefix 'uj' attached to verbs and nouns, means upwards or superiority in rank. It also means blowing or expanding. It conveys the sense of pre-eminence and power. Jaya means conquest, victory, triumph or success. Ujjayi is the process in which the lungs are fully expanded and the chest puffed out like that of a proud conqueror. This type of pranayama aerates the lungs, removes phlegm, gives endurance, soothes the nerves and tones the entire system. Ujjayi without kumbhaka, done in a reclining position, is ideal for persons suffering from high blood pressure or coronary troubles.

Kapalabhati Pranayama

The process of Kapalabhati is a milder form of Bhastrika Pranayama. In this pranayama, the inhalation is slow but the exhalation is vigorous. There is a split second of retention after each exhalation. Both Bhastrika and Kapalabhati activate and invigorate the liver, spleen, pancreas and abdominal muscles. Thus digestion is improved, the sinuses are drained, the eyes feel cool and one has a general sense of exhilaration.

Anuloma–Viloma Pranayama

The Viloma and Anuloma types of Pranayama are concerned with the methods and techniques of inhalation and exhalation. In Viloma, the inhalation or exhalation is not one continuous process, but is done gradually with several pauses. In Anuloma, inhalation is through both nostrils as in Ujjayi and exhalation is alternate through either nostril as in

Nadi Sodhana. Viloma Pranayama in the first stage helps those suffering from low blood pressure. In the second stage it benefits persons suffering from high blood pressure.

Sitali Pranayama

Sitala means cool. This pranayama cools the system, hence the name. It soothes the eyes and ears. It is beneficial in cases of low fever and biliousness. It activates the liver and the spleen, improves digestion and relieves thirst.

Sitkari Pranayama

Sitakari is that which causes cold. This is a variation of Sitali Pranayama. The effects are the same as those mentioned for Sitali Pranayama.

Bibliography

Every Diet Is Worth a Try

1. Martin Katahn, *The Rotation Diet*, W.W. Norton & Company, 2012.
2. Rujuta Diwekar, *Don't Lose Your Mind, Lose Your Weight*, first edition Random House India, 2009; reprinted Penguin Random House, Ebury Press, 2011.
3. Calorie counter:www.webmd.com (healthtool, exercise, calculator).

Inside Outside

1. Harriet Brown, *Brave Girl Eating: A Family's Struggle With Anorexia,* HarperCollins, 2010.
2. Kelsey Osgood, *How to Disappear Completely:*

On Modern Anorexia, Duckworth Overlook, 2014.
3. Dr Scott C. Litin, ed., *Mayo Clinic Family Health Book*, 5th edition, Mayo Clinic, 2018.

The Smoking Gun and Other Addictions

1. D. Croydon Hammond, ed., *Handbook of Hypnotic Suggestions and Metaphors,* An American Society of Clinical Hypnosis Book, W.W. Norton, 1990; https://www.verywellmind.com.

Finding Dance and Yoga

1. B.K.S. Iyengar, *Light on Yoga*, Allen & Unwin, 1968.
2. B.K.S. Iyengar, *Yoga: The Path to Holistic Health*, Dorling Kindersley, 2007.

The Empty Sella

1. https://en.m.wikipedia.org.

Training Tiny Muscles

1. Pierre Sollier, *Listening for Wellness: An Introduction to the Tomatis Method*, The Mozart Center Press, 2005.

A Coloured Life

1. Edwin Babbitt, *The Principles of Light and Color*, https://library.si.edu–Books.
2. Samina T. Yousef Azeemi, S. Mohsin Raza, 'A Critical Analysis of Chromotherapy and Its Scientific Evolution', 2005, https://www.ncbi.nim.nih.gov, www.hindawi.com, Evidence-Based Complementary and Alternative Medicine, Volume 2, Article ID 254639.
3. https://www.sciencedirect.com/science/article/abs/pii/S1011134413002881.
4. https://www.researchgate.net/publication/226798260_Photon_Sucking_as_an_Essential_Principle_of_Biological_Regulation.
5. https://www.springer.com/gp/book/9780792350828.
6. https://pubmed.ncbi.nlm.nih.gov/15244259/.
7. https://www.aan.com/PressRoom/Home/PressRelease/3777.
8. https://presse.inserm.fr/le-travail-de-nuit-un-risque-pour-les-femmes/1300/.
9. Rakesh Gupta, 'Color Therapy in Mental Health and Well Being', *International Journal of All Research Education and Scientific Methods*, Volume 9, Issue 2, February, 2021, Central

Council for Research In Yoga and Naturopathy, New Delhi. (IJARESM, ISSN: 2455-6211, Impact Factor: 7.429, Available online at: www.ijaresm.com) corroborates Chakra theory with colours).

Mudslinging

1. Anjou Musafir and Pascal Chazot, *Clay Cures: Nature's Miracle for the New Age*, Mapin Publishing, 2006.
2. Lynda B. Williams and Shelley E. Haydel, 'Evaluation of the medicinal use of clay minerals as antibacterial agents', PubMed Central, US National Library of Medicine.

With a Little Help from My Friends

1. Fumiko Takatsu, *The Ultimate Guide to the Face Yoga Method: Take Five Years Off Your Face*, CreateSpace Independent Publishing Platform, 2013.

Healing Others

1. Choa Kok Sui, *The Ancient Science and Art of Pranic Healing*, Institute for Inner Studies, Inc., 1987.

2. Choa Kok Sui, *Advanced Pranic Healing*, Institute for Inner Studies, Inc., 2012

Unmessing My Head

1. Marshall B. Rosenberg, Deepak Chopra, *Nonviolent Communication: A Language of Life*, Puddle Dancer Press, 2015.
2. Lucy Leu, *Nonviolent Communication Companion Workbook*, Banyan Tree, 2016.
3. Marshall B. Rosenberg, *Being Me, Loving You: A Practical Guide To Extraordinary Relationships*, Puddle Dancer Press, 2005; https://www.bayareanvc.org.
4. Allan Rohlfs, *Beyond Anger and Blame: How to Achieve Constructive Conflict,* pub. *The Christian Century Magazine*, 2012.
5. Marion Little, 'Total Honesty/Total Heart: Fostering Empathy Development and Conflict Resolution Skills', MA thesis, University of Victoria, 2008.

ALSO IN SPEAKING TIGER

ONE FOOT ON THE GROUND
A Life Told Through the Body

Shanta Gokhale

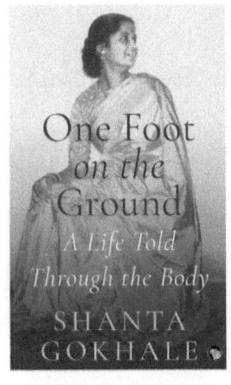

In this unusual, extraordinary autobiography, Shanta Gokhale—writer, translator and one of India's most illuminating cultural commentators—traces the arc of her life over eight decades through the progress of her body, as it grows, matures and begins to wind down. Starting with her birth in 1939—in philosophic silence, till the doctor's slap on her bottom made her bawl—she recounts her childhood, youth and middle and old age in chapters built around the many elements and processes of the physical self: tonsils and adenoids, breasts and misaligned teeth; childbirth and fluctuating weight, cancer and bunions. And through these memories emerge others, less visible but just as defining: a carefree childhood growing up in a progressive Marathi household in Mumbai's Shivaji Park; the pleasures, in adolescence, of badminton, Kathak and hairdressing; the warmth of friends and an almost love in cold England; finding and losing a mate—twice—and bringing up her children as a single parent; the great thrill of her first translation from Marathi into English; nursing her mother, dying of cancer, as she would a baby; surviving cancer herself, and writing her second novel through the recovery.

Told with effortless humour and candour, *One Foot on the Ground* is the story of a life full of happiness, heartbreak, wonder and acceptance. It will rank among the finest personal histories written in India.

ALSO IN SPEAKING TIGER

BIG BHISHMA IN MADRAS
In Search of *The Mahabharata* with Peter Brook

Jean-Claude Carriere

Translated from the French by Aruna Vasudev

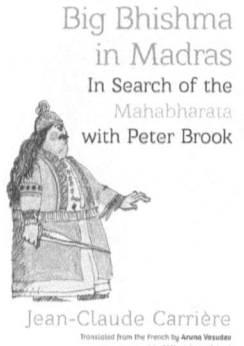

A chance comment in 1974 fired Peter Brook and Jean-Claude Carriere with the idea of producing a play based on the epic. Together they travelled across India, searching for all possible theatrical forms of the great poem. The result was an epic play—9 hours with two intermissions—later made into a film and a TV series, which has become a landmark in theatre. Another result was this delightful book made from the notes that Carriere jotted down during his travels, whose charm is enhanced by his piquant illustrations that run through the pages.

The 'sacred frenzy' of Theyyam in a Kerala village and the intricacies of Kathakali are interwoven with their encounters with the aged Shankaracharya of Kanchipuram, a 'one-in-three', and the legendary Satyajit Ray in Kolkata. Here they also meet Professor P. Lal, who has been working for twenty years on translating the *Mahabharata* into English. It is vignettes like these that make their search for the epic into a journey that shows India, through Carriere's words and sketches, in a way it has never been seen before.

Stylish Amma in dark glasses, with Kartikeya and me on holiday in Venice, 1958.

(Below): Papa ordering hot chocolate for me at a café in Venice, 1958.

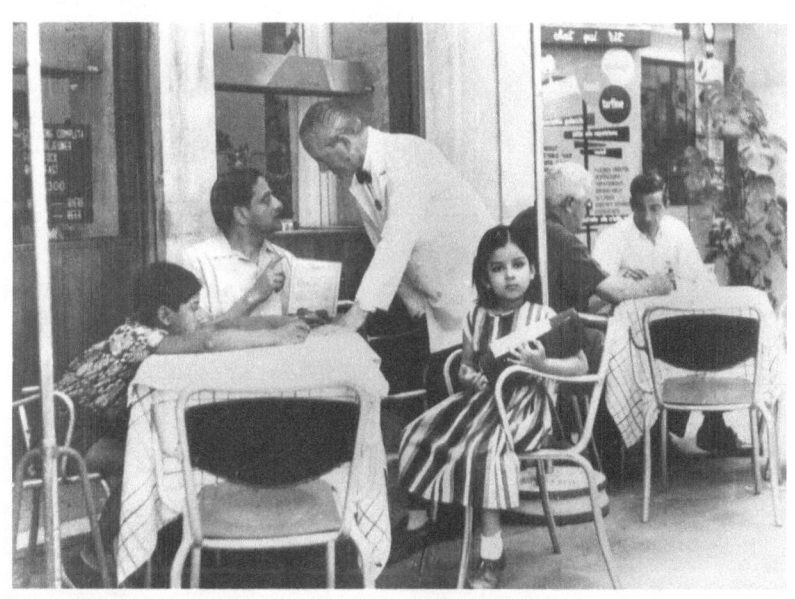

All images except where specified courtesy the author.

In Amma's sitting room with my aunt, Capt. Lakshmi Sehgal (of the Indian National Army), my CPML cousin Srilata Swaminathan, Amma, (*seated, right to left*), Anahita and Kartikeya.

Three generations in Madras: With Amma on the porch of my grandmother Ammu Swaminathan in Chetput, Gilchrist Gardens 1968. Ammaji in the background.

Amma, Revanta, Anahita and me with Tipki our Dalmation and Sukhi, our Dobergirl, in my sitting room at Darpana, 1998.

Practicing to participate in a college youth festival, 1973.

With Amma in rehearsal, 1990, when she started teaching me the rare gems of the Pandanallur Bharatanatyam repertoire that she had learned from her gurus.

Rehearsing for a Darpana Annual Day. I am fifth from the left, and seem the only one not taking it very seriously!

Amma's last year: In her sitting room, with an Angkor Vat rubbing of Lord Kartikeya on the wall behind us, 2015. Photo: Vivek Desai

Still from *Mena Gurjari* with co-star Rajeev, 1976. The film ran to full houses for 52 weeks.

Playing a 70-year-old in Malayali film director T.V. Chandran's film, *Danny*, 2001.

Modelling a gown from Wendell Rodrigue's 'range to dance' series.
Photo: Rafique Sayed

Modelling in a jumpsuit. I look at this photograph and wonder why I thought I was fat! Photo: Dheeraj Chavda

Dancing in a white dress, 2005. At my cottage on the farm where I tried organic farming. Celebrations in the evening meant swimming and dancing.

Performing the Bhamakalapam in Kuchipudi.

From my dance piece, 'Structures', 1995, with music by Toshi Tsuchitori who had composed the music for *The Mahabharata*.

From the production, 'The Colours of Her Heart', which I worked on with British Pakistani singer Samia Malik. This is from the Seattle performance in 2019, directed by Yadavan Chandran. Photo: Eric Richmond

Role of a lifetime:
As Draupadi in Peter Brook's
The Mahabharata.
Photos: Gilles Abegg

www.ingramcontent.com/pod-product-compliance
Lightning Source LLC
LaVergne TN
LVHW041925070526
838199LV00051BA/2723